# FACING DEPRESSION

**Books by Michael Lawson**

Facing Anxiety and Stress (*Hodder and Stoughton*)
The Unfolding Kingdom (*Kingsway*)
Sex and That (*Lion*)
Cautionary Tales (*Marshall Pickering*)

# FACING DEPRESSION

Michael Lawson

**HODDER AND STOUGHTON**
LONDON SYDNEY AUCKLAND TORONTO

All Bible quotations are taken from the New International Version, copyright © 1973, 1978, 1984 by International Bible Society. Published by Hodder & Stoughton Limited. Used by permission.

**British Library Cataloguing in Publication Data**

Lawson, Michael, 1952–
    Facing depression.
    1. Man. Depression, Christian viewpoints
    I. Title
    261.5'15

    ISBN 0-340-42687-x

# CONTENTS

# FOREWORD

Michael Lawson's book is written for a wide readership, for roughly one in four people face depression at some stage in their adult life. Those who escape this condition are likely to know, among family or friends, at least one person whose day-to-day functioning is disrupted by a depressive illness. Depression is no respecter of persons: men and women, young and old, people of different races and cultures, rich and poor, the obscure and the famous, can all be afflicted by this miserable and saddening state. Robert Schumann, the composer, battled with melancholy; Winston Churchill fought against the ravages of what he called his 'Black Dog'; and many well-known comedians suffer from what has been described as 'smiling' depression. In the world of fiction too, few scenes are quite complete without the presence of someone who displays elements of depression. We immediately recognise, for example, the state of mind in Marvin, the humanoid robot in Douglas Adams' *The Hitch Hiker's Guide to the Galaxy*, who reveals a depressive personality in his slow deliberations, monotonous voice and heavily negative views.

*Facing Depression* is a book which will help many who try to cope with depressed feelings, as well as people who seek to understand and care for those so afflicted. Readers will find the wisdom of these pages factual, practical and scriptural.

Michael Lawson tackles the hard facts about depression in a business-like and straightforward way. Although he avoids technical language he has given a faithful account of the 'nuts and bolts' of the condition – including descriptions of the variety of forms of depression, as well as its possible causes and range of treatments. In doing this, he gives graphic examples of real life situations, in which men and women struggle to find their way in life's darker stretches.

It is the practicality of this book that is outstanding. So much that is written on stress, anxiety and depression is good on the 'whats' and the 'whys' but not on the 'how tos'. Here Michael Lawson spells out a series of questions and exercises for self-reflection and prayer. I, for one, have found these both searching and encouraging. Further, he gives many clear guidelines to enable the reader to move forward in terms of self-understanding and overcoming attitudes and behaviour which block the way ahead.

Thirdly, we have here a piece of writing that is thoroughly scriptural. The author avoids the extremes of dropping proof-texts like unexploded bombs in the reader's path and confusing the route forward with complicated and clever theological argument. We find instead the heartfelt anguish of the psalmist, the perplexed musings of Job, the 'burn out' of the exhausted Elijah and the fear in the face of life's trials among those Christians who received the Letter to the Hebrews. Michael Lawson gently draws out lessons for today's troubled women and men as he explores the pages of Scripture.

Christians often polarise their views on depression in two major areas – those of cause and treatment. In the first, there is an inclination either to argue that depression is invariably the outcome of sin or to see the condition on a purely medical footing. In the second, help is viewed as essentially one of repentance and a new resolve to obey the Lord or in terms of taking the right tablets under the right supervision. This is where Michael Lawson, in avoiding these oversimplifications, has written such a useful book. There are many reasons why a person becomes depressed – including the loss of a loved one, being out of work, coping with long-term illness, suppressing feelings of anger, trying to live with unresolved conflict and a response to some genetic and biochemical tendency. As a result there is a wide range of ways of finding relief: from talking with a friend to sharing with a counsellor; from joining a self-help group to seeking psychiatric advice;

from receiving and giving forgiveness to strategies for new ways of thinking and behaving. In all these advances the Lord himself is the one who brings challenge, solace, and enabling. As Michael Lawson puts it:

The world is a painful place. But whatever the appearances, it is not finally out of control, and God is not too distant to come to our aid. Jesus has the final authority. We need to know that when we are up against it. It is not an impersonal universe. There is love in the person of Jesus right at the centre (chapter 7, page 108).

Dr Roger F. Hurding

# AUTHOR'S PREFACE

It is important that a book on Depression finds its proper audience. *Facing Depression* is a self-help book. It is designed to assist different people at different points of need. It has certainly been written for those who are either presently facing depression, or who have been through the experience in the past. There are many practical, psychological and spiritual elements here which will aid in the learning process of self strengthening against further depressive episodes. Someone who is just entering or leaving a depressive period will, of course, find it easier to manage a book like this than those who are at their lowest point.

This is also a book for those who want to help a friend, relation, or colleague. There are many exercises in these pages which are an essential part of making what is contained here as effective as possible in helping those who are depressed or subject to depression. Please don't skimp them, they contain keys to your freedom.

This book is written from the conviction that Jesus Christ is the central explanation of our lives and the universe we live in. Nonetheless, much of what is described here will be of real benefit to those for whom faith in Jesus Christ is not yet a living reality; but the help which comes from God is so richly powerful it cannot be discounted in a book of this type.

Depression affects the mind, the body and the spirit. One can be treated to the neglect of another. The Church and the medical profession are both guilty of such imbalance from time to time. The aim here, however, is not to be narrowly selective. A great number of books on depression have one exclusive theory, and say 'you follow my road and I'll get you there'. They help some, but not many. Here the approach is far more eclectic. All truth is God's truth, and so the insights are drawn from a wide variety of sources, including my own experience and training in counselling, both secular and Christian. The intention is to see all these elements within a truly biblical world view.

My heartfelt concern and prayer as I have written these pages, is that those who face depression will find here a sympathetic approach, involving practical understanding, a deeper self knowledge, and spiritual insight and strength to help them overcome the very painful and disorientating experience of depression. Recognising and facing the underlying issues lies at the heart of this approach. I have known so many who have overcome their difficulties in this way, through taking the principles described in *Facing Depression* wholly into their lives.

Part One

# The Nature of Depression

# 1

# THE EXPERIENCE OF DEPRESSION

Being depressed is more than feeling fed up. It is more even than just the occasional attack of the blues. Those moments when they come are unwelcome enough, of course, and we would all prefer not to have them; but real depression is a far more gloomy experience.

Have you ever felt you are:

* slowing down
* getting muzzy headed
* anxious and nervous
* irritable or agitated
* feeling low about yourself
* useless and without hope
* deeply guilty about wrong thoughts and actions
* sinking into the depths of despair

Have you noticed:

* interruption to your normal sleep pattern
* much less energy to cope
* continual tiredness
* unusual aches and pains
* changes to your appetite and body weight
* difficulty in contributing to conversations
* fear of meeting people

Feelings such as these make you feel wretched and definitely not yourself. You are out of sorts in a big way. You know it, and the experience is as painful as it is bewildering. Of course, you do not have to experience all these signs and symptoms to be depressed – just a few is enough for most people.

A 25-year-old shop assistant put her feelings about her depressed state into words which many in this situation echo in their own experience.

'What is happening to the bottom of my life? It seems to be dropping out! I feel unsettled about myself. I'm sleeping badly. Sometimes I feel guilty. I really don't like myself much, and I'm sure others find me difficult and boring. I'm tired, I'm tearful. Life is just one uphill struggle . . .'

## The characteristics of depression

Many of us will have times when we feel sad about something, but sadness is not the same as depression. When we are feeling off-colour, we may say we are depressed, we really mean we are tired, or bored, or just plain fed up.

Real depression usually involves five characteristics, all of which inter-relate and affect each other:

* A sense of inner emptiness and barrenness, rather than general sadness, is a dominant emotion.
* Energy levels become noticeably depleted.
* The normal sense of humour is vastly diminished, being replaced by self pity.
* Negative thoughts and feelings predominate, concerning self, others and the future.
* Renunciation takes over, involving the giving up of responsibility for self, any desire to get the best out of life, and eventually hope for the future. In serious cases of psychosis even the ability to discern reality is relinquished.

These five characteristics of depression are found in all depressive states. There are many other visible signs, like alteration to your sleep pattern, which are important diagnostically, but these are the main characteristics.

## Varied origins

Reacting to something painful, either in the present, or in the past, is the most common kind of depression we encounter. Sometimes there is not an obvious psychological or spiritual cause to the depression. But depression can also come from within, and be a medical phenomenon, either partly or wholly. The chemistry of our brain cells affects our moods and the way we feel, and those subtle chemical balances and reactions within our brains can become disordered through illness. Though the symptoms of such disorders are very similar to reactive depression, it is essential that such endogenous depression, as it is often termed, receives adequate medical attention. As always, it is a matter of accurately matching the treatment to need. There are some things you simply cannot talk yourself out of.

A brilliant young musician was unable to perform for several months in the year because of disabling and recurrent bouts of black depression. No amount of talking to wise friends and skilful counsellors seemed to make any significant difference. When he was eventually persuaded by his doctor to try a course of drug therapy, he was doubtful about the likelihood of improvement. It was explained that there are forms of depression which are illnesses in their own right, and appropriate medical treatments are the only effective way of handling them. Today, that same musician has a full, active life and an outstanding and uninterrupted playing career.

The experience of depression takes many forms, and not everyone faces exactly the same set of feelings and impressions of what is happening to them. One fact, nonetheless, is universal: no one enjoys it. It is a deeply unhappy experience for everybody. Strangely, when depressed, you always feel a kind of isolation, as though you are the only person to have suffered this. Sometimes you do not think it is depression at all, you just imagine you are losing your grip. It can seem like that, but the facts may tell a different story. Many millions of good, able and otherwise healthy people have become depressed at some point in their lives. If you are facing such a time at present, then be assured, you are not alone; and there is much which can be done to help.

Though the experience of depression is painful, dark, and with time becomes increasingly hopeless and alienating, this sense of isolation can be an even more crippling and burdensome feature of this sense of dis-ease, than some of its other manifestations. The person suffering from depression needs a restored perspective, and a renewed hope. In part, this can be helped by seeing that others suffer too. There is no shame in being depressed, for many ordinary people suffer for very ordinary reasons. Isolation should be dealt with; by talking with trusted friends and helpers; and by learning from the experience of others as to how they have suffered and overcome.

## A question of brain power

There is a great deal of activity going on all the time, twenty-four hours a day, every day, in the ten thousand million nerve cells of our remarkably complex and wonderfully designed human brain. We all know that thoughts and feelings are available both for immediate use and for future reference, carefully filed and sorted by our brain's intricate storage and retrieval mechanisms. Freudian psychology has made us actively aware of the existence of the conscious and the unconscious dimensions of the human mind. What many of us are far less aware of is the powerful activity going on every moment, day and night, at the physical rather than psychological level of the brain's functioning.

Whatever else, externally and within, which may contribute to our experience of mood – being up or down, happy or unhappy, thrilled or disappointed – the final mechanism in making those moods a felt reality is the complex chemistry by which our brain functions. The normal work of our brain's chemistry is to ensure that we receive the right 'mood messages' – from our thoughts and reactions. It is like a conductor interpreting a musical score. If the message in the music is fast and furious, then the conductor creates a corresponding mood of frenzied activity; if it is warm and tender, then an atmosphere lovingly romantic. Our brain chemistry interprets the mood messages of our thoughts and actions, and as such, like the conductor in relation to the musical score, it is the last link in the chain. This is simply the way we have been made – the Creator's remarkably intricate design to enable us to function daily, with all the possibilities and potential of the richness of felt experience that life has to offer.

## Tell me the whole story

When we say our moods are controlled by chemical activity within us, we are not saying that is the whole story, any more than a conductor could do without the music! What we are saying is that God has made us to be a unity of body, mind and spirit. And though many of us jump to the conclusion that depression is more to do with the mind and spirit, in fact we need to take into account the physical aspects too, if we want to have a rounded and complete picture of what may be going on. We sometimes find that one area of our being may need more attention than another.

Of course, just as our bodies are subject to decay and disease, so, unfortunately, are our minds. Since mood is controlled by way of the neurones of our brains, it is equally possible for illness to afflict our mental life; and this is certainly so in endogenous depression.

## The chemistry of feelings

The human brain is a wonder of complexity, and it is valuable to know something more about the way it has been designed and the manner in which it functions.

Moment by moment, constant electrical messages pass to and fro as moods, thoughts, sensations and feelings are unceasingly monitored, formulated and expressed. There are approximately eight thousand interconnections which conduct small electric charges between the ten thousand million nerve cells or neurones. Such an electric charge passes from the head to the tail of the cell, coming to rest amidst the thousands of terminal buttons. Between those terminal buttons and the head of the next cell exist microscopic gaps called synapses. It is not possible for the charge to jump the synaptic gap, instead it causes a chemical change to take place within the synapse so causing a new charge to commence in the head of the next cell.

The chemicals which in effect transfer an electric charge from one neurone to the next are called neurotransmitters. Many neurotransmitters exist, but a group thought to be especially important in the regulation of mood are known as monoamines or catecholamines. One factor in depression is believed by some theorists to be connected with the depletion or reduction in activity of brain monoamine transmitters, which leads to a depressing effect on mood. It is certainly true that disorders of brain chemistry are linked in some complex ways with depressive states as with other conditions which affect both mind and behaviour; though it is by no means clear in precise terms how all these different elements work together.

## Blinded by science

Although there is still much discussion, many researchers on the subject are agreed there are basically two groups of depression with varying degrees of overlap. They are known as reactive and endogenous depression. There are also psychological, spiritual and existential elements in depressive states and illness, but these are really part of the reactive group, so they do not properly figure here as separate categories.

You are now probably suitably blinded by science. Don't worry about the unfamiliar terms, they are only labels on the bottle, even though they may sound like foreign sounding wines! It is important to understand what they mean. So here is a simple basic explanation of what each one signifies, to take some of the mystery out of it.

## Reactive depression

The word 'reactive' itself suggests some kind of reaction to an event or set of events which in some way provokes a depressive response. Jane, a single woman in her fifties, had spent many years in a friendly and supportive church, in a community which she knew and loved. When her elderly sister became ill, it became necessary for Jane to uproot, and leave her own home and move to another part of the country to go and care for her sister. Well-adjusted to the idea of helping her sister as she was, all that Jane lost in terms of her friends, familiar places, and the comfort and privacy of her own home took its toll. Jane found it hard to account for the depressed feelings and slowness of mind she began to experience some months after her move. It was a kind of bereavement, for Jane was understandably reacting against her loss.

We all feel mildly fed up when faced with unexpected bills, or an unpleasant experience of some kind. We are reacting to an event, but we usually soon adjust and the mood passes. But there are some events, either in the present or in the past, which make a more powerful impact on our sensitive inner selves. Reaction to a cause is the basic principle here.

All of us are different, so what may affect one person may have little effect on another. It seems to be the case where real depression is concerned (that is when there is a continuous and seriously marked depression of mood and other mental and physical functioning) that the reaction is often to some kind of loss experience. It doesn't have to be, but loss of some kind or another is a common component in this kind of reactive phase. The loss acts as a sort of trigger, setting off the reaction in mood, physical responses and behaviour, leaving the sufferer feeling largely debilitated and out of sorts.

This kind of loss reaction can take on a number of different forms. Bereavement, of course, is one poignant example. Bereavement is often thought of as only referring to the death of loved ones. That kind of loss is particularly painful. But, as we have seen in Jane's situation, painful experiences of this kind can equally be to do with other kinds of loss: a pet perhaps, or the departure of a friend or relative to another part of the country or abroad. Similarly loss can be experienced in terms of self esteem, perhaps experienced through retirement or redundancy.

Sometimes in personal relationships loss can be experienced most severely when a relationship breaks down, and there is a separation or divorce. Equally loss can just as much be experienced materially. We are physical beings, so no wonder we get attached to material things. Of such an order are financial losses, the loss of a specially valued object, or the loss of a house or flat. For some reason all these losses can and do form the basis in some people of painful reactive depression. They are the trigger which sets the whole mechanism to work. There are, however, in addition, other triggers of considerable importance such as interpersonal conflict, stress, extreme anxiety and other factors which function in a similar way.

## Endogenous depression

When people say 'it is all in the mind', it may be more accurate to say it is all in the brain. As creatures made in the image of God we have been fashioned as physical beings, and there can be disorders which affect our mood, just as much as there are other disorders which affect other parts of our make-up.

There is an area of depression which can be traced back precisely to this area of what is going on chemically in the brain. We have noted the brain's intricately designed mechanisms, enabling us to do and experience a phenomenal variety of richness in mood, activity and awareness. In the area of mood a subtle balance is achieved by the brain's precise chemistry that very occasionally becomes upset, consequently affecting our sense of mental and emotional equilibrium. Such a form of depression is termed 'endogenous', from a Greek word meaning 'from within'. The cause is internal rather than external. This is an illness in its own right, and a recognisable condition. In the last few years enormous strides have been made in the treatment of endogenous depression, so that all but the very severest sufferers can lead a perfectly normal life.

## Ups and downs

One form of the illness may exhibit swings of mood to an exaggerated degree. Mania can sound an extreme word to use, but it only refers to this exaggerated 'high' mood swing. Sometimes someone will feel perhaps uncharacteristically the life and soul of the party. They will be cracking jokes here, there and everywhere. Spending sprees, wise or unwise, will suddenly become the order of the day. It can be more extreme than that too, involving what used to be called delusions of grandeur! Such experience can be followed by particularly low phases; gloomy, sad, slow minded times.

These are the 'ups and downs', the highs and lows characteristic of manic depressive psychosis.

This bi-polar or manic depressive illness is not uncom-
mon, particularly amongst gifted able and active people. The
composer, Robert Schumann, the British Prime Minister, Sir
Winston Churchill, and many other famous names are all
said to have suffered this illness. Some of the greatest creative
artists the world has ever known have been manic depressives. Some people can be very ill indeed with such an illness;
it is a condition with a wide spectrum of degrees of severity.
The severest sufferers can lose touch with reality altogether
for extended periods, and this is known as a psychotic state.

Much progress has been made, so that today, much is
understood about this illness, and tremendous strides forward have been made in its treatment. It is possible too to
'suffer' from a cyclothymic personality. This is a person
whose mood swings regularly up and down without the
extremes of manic-depressive syndrome, but this is not an
illness as such. Those with this component to their personal
make-up are more prone to depressive illness of this type.

Endogenous depression may also be 'unipolar' in form.
That is to have just the low experiences without any symptoms of elation. However, the symptoms of elation do not
have to be very extreme or frequent to be symptoms of manic
depression. Whatever the diagnosis, and only a doctor or
psychiatrist can diagnose and treat this particular form
properly (though others can give effective support in addition), endogenous depression definitely does not mean you
are mad, or anything of the sort. You can be helped. In a
sense a purely physical illness is more straightforward to
treat than a complex psychological one, and preventative
treatment can sometimes be given to stop it recurring.

## It's my glands, doctor

There are in addition several general illnesses which can
precipitate or exacerbate depressive conditions. Some viral

infections have this kind of effect and the depression will sometimes outlast by many months the original infection. Influenza, viral hepatitis and glandular fever are all of this order.

Many hormones have an effect on mood, including those from the hypothalmus, pituitary gland, adrenal glands, thyroid glands, parathyroid glands and pancreas, as well as female sexual hormones. Hormones are chemical messengers which regulate the activities of certain parts of the body. There is normally a rise in the hormone, progesterone, in the female menstrual cycle. Lower levels of progesterone have been measured in women who suffer from pre-menstrual tension, which often includes depression. Diseases of these glands, such as Hypopituitarism, Addison's disease, Cushing's syndrome, Hypothyroidism, Hyperparathyroidism, Diabetes Mellitus, Cancer of the intestine and pancreas, as well as Organic brain disease and Anaemia are also known in a few cases to be linked with depressive symptoms. Such occurrences may be relatively rare, but they show again the vital and dynamic inter-relationship between mind and body. Depression can also form a part of growing up, the change of life, and growing old. There is always a further possibility that some drugs may precipitate depression as a side effect.

## Maternity blues

Fifty per cent of women experience mild depression following childbirth, starting on the second or third day and usually lasting for only a few days. About ten per cent of mothers face rather more severe depression after the birth, either quite soon or after some weeks. This can last months or a year, with certain cases of more prolonged suffering. Post natal or puerperal psychosis, affecting only three in every thousand women is a serious, though fairly rare complication, often with symptoms of paranoia, blackness of mood and other deeply distressing elements.

## Suicide

Between fifty and seventy-five per cent of those who kill themselves are clinically depressed. It is therefore vital to take seriously any talk of suicide in any form, even though it may only turn out to be an exercise in self attention on the part of the manipulative depressee. After traffic accidents, suicide is the most frequent cause of death in young men. One study suggests that ten per cent of patients who have received hospital treatment for severe depression eventually kill themselves.

Attempted suicide, or parasuicide as it is sometimes known, is of a different order of concern to genuine suicidal tendencies. The parasuicide often wants only to have a break from oppressive stress, to draw attention to their need for help, sometimes simply to gain attention, or to get their own back by hurting someone who has hurt them. Sixty per cent of parasuicides claim they meant to kill themselves, though this is probably more to do with face saving than morbid intentions.

## Hints or warnings of suicide

Suicidal talk should always be taken with seriousness, even though you may have real cause to doubt someone's intentions. Even half serious attempts go wrong sometimes, and angry gestures can end up in tragedy. Watch out for the signs which give an indication that all is not well. A combination of the following is worth taking seriously.

*Signs*

The person may speak of their desire to die, or give direct warnings of their intentions. Hints can be more than verbal. If there is a sudden interest in tidying up personal affairs, or an accumulation of medicines or alcohol, or something else which could be used to take life then this is the time for serious action.

## Drug abuse and alcohol

Those who abuse drugs and alcohol, are those who find coping with stress particularly difficult. If there has been a particular trauma, such as a relationship breakdown, then this is a time of considerable risk.

## Bereavement

Losing a close relative, such as a spouse, or a mother losing an only son is a high risk factor. If the person concerned is a dependent personality, then the risk is all the greater.

## Isolation

Illness, bereavement, and unemployment lead to loneliness and isolation. This can vastly accentuate the sense of hopelessness and despair which depression can bring.

## Variation in depressive mood

If there are strong feelings of meaninglessness, guilt, or unworthiness then there is a risk of suicidal thoughts. In the blackest moods the person may not have enough energy to 'organise' themselves for suicide. The time to watch is when there is a partial upswing in mood, especially if the person suddenly appears cheerful and settled, yet somehow distant in their manner.

## Previous attempts

Suicide is a hundred times more likely amongst those who have previously attempted suicide than the rest of the population. Watch situations where a previous attempt was

violent in any way, or involved an attempt to disguise the fact
of attempted suicide.

## Close up on you

Correct diagnosis is essential if we are to get the treatment for
depression right. Do be clear about this. There is so much
which can be done to help depression. And if you are a
sufferer, you may feel at the desperate stage – hang on for
there is help at hand.

Have you got round to telling someone how you feel yet?
You may have any number of thoughts about that. Perhaps
you feel embarrassed or stupid about it? You may feel you
ought to be able to get a grip on yourself? Maybe you think
you'll lose face in the eyes of someone whose respect you
particularly value, if you tell them what is going on? The
answer to all these questions is that it is very important
indeed to have the support of those who understand us; and it
only makes things worse to have to hide ourselves from others
and bottle things up. So many millions of people suffer from
depression, including many Christians. There is definitely no
shame in it. You don't have to be isolated. Just telling a
compassionate friend can remove tremendous burdens.
Don't be a lone yachtsman. Go and tell someone.

## The way ahead

It is time now to move forward on two fronts. They are to do
with knowing yourself and knowing God. The task is to
spend some moments noting down exactly how you feel at the
moment; thinking about anything you can remember which
may affect your present situation. Then bring those thoughts
to God in prayer, and ask his help to get you moving forward

and find freedom from the sadness and difficulties you have been facing.

A pencil and paper, and a quiet place, will help as you try and answer these questions about yourself, noting your answers down as simply as you can.

* Try to put into words how you have been feeling and for how long you've felt like this.
* Have you noticed any other changes in yourself or your normal pattern of life?
* Is there anything worrying you in particular?
* Are you able to do anything about it?
* Of all the things you are feeling, is there one which is most unsettling?
* What are the most painful and possibly formative experiences of your past?
* Is there some painful past event or situation which may have something to do with your present feelings?
* Is there something that could happen which would really make a difference to the way you feel now?

When you have done that, the chances are that you may well have a much clearer picture of what may be going on within you. If you have found an answer to what can actually be done to help, then, if it is within your power, do try and contribute to it working out. Remember, if you tell someone else then they may be able to help and assist you too.

Ultimately, our help comes from God himself. So before you do anything it will be good to pray over these findings, and ask his strength as you go on further to face the underlying issues of depression, and find a real way forward. Don't lose that piece of paper, you need it now, but you'll need it later on as well.

When you can be quiet and alone, read this verse from Psalm 145 which reminds us of God's care. He is close to us.

He understands us. And he is simply waiting for us to bring our needs to him.

> The Lord is near to all who call on him, to all who call on him in truth.          [Psalm 145:18]

If it helps, use this outline of a prayer to bring your needs and the findings you have just noted to your Heavenly Father. You can either pray it as it stands, or use it as a starting off point for your own praying. Tell God either silently or out loud just how you feel, and what is going through your mind. He understands; he cares; and he wants to help you.

> Thank you Heavenly Father that you are near and you do care. Having thought about myself and the way I've been just recently, I realise I need your help and your healing. I bring before you, Lord, what I have discovered about myself. Where there has been wrong, I seek your pardon. I thank you that Jesus Christ brings complete forgiveness, however large or small our sins may be. So I seek that forgiveness, and redirect my life in your ways for the future. When I feel wretched, low or helpless, please assure me again of your loving presence. And when the tunnel seems darkest, remind me once more that it is but a prelude to freedom, which the light of your healing will bring me. So I ask for your strength and upholding. Help me Lord to take on all that is necessary for that work of healing to be completed. Please grant me your peace – in and through Jesus Christ. Amen.

# 2

# WHY WE GET DEPRESSED

If we can only find out the cause, we'll be halfway towards a cure. When applied to depression, this commonly held maxim has much to commend it. Because there are different kinds of depression, it is important to try and decide which form or mix of elements in depression we are dealing with. This will give clues to the cause, and hence the best way of handling it. Right diagnosis is always the prelude to cure.

## Three real life studies

*Reaction to change?*

Jean is forty-nine, and happily married to David. They have three children: Tim, eighteen; Graham, sixteen; and Jane, fourteen. Jean has been a reasonably steady person all her adult life, both in raising the family and helping David run a small business, the Post Office and newsagents in the High Street of the quiet northern town in which they live.

Like most parents, Jean feels the changes and pressures brought on by the children's teenage years considerably. Jean has been particularly concerned about Tim, their eldest son, whose assertions of independence have led to several family disagreements and personal anxiety for Jean herself in recent weeks. But the pain of these growing years has heightened dramatically in these last few days. News of Tim's girlfriend's pregnancy has knocked Jean sideways. On her own admission, Jean responded badly at first. Later she felt guilty at her reaction. She wished she had been more constructive when she had heard the news, instead of flaring up as she had; but it had all come as the climax to a simply terrible week, and Jean's energy and patience were slipping away fast.

Family matters are not at all happy at the moment. Graham's laziness at school is putting his future in jeopardy. In this same week, Jane has been caught by the police, drinking under-age at the disco in town. It is quite a culmination of events. So Tim's news, coming on top of everything else is simply the worst possible.

Jean's reaction to all this is not exactly what David had expected of her. Jean had good reason to be angry and her normal response under stress is a mildly explosive one-off expression of her feelings – a few cross words and that is it. It has been this way for twenty-two years. But things are noticeably different this time.

Jean isn't sleeping at all well, and the days are quite a struggle too. The evenings are the worst time. There's a gnawing sense of anxiety, an unsettling irritability, even tears when David isn't watching. Jean doesn't want David to think there is something wrong; that she isn't coping; that she is coming to the end of her tether. She feels such a failure. But David knows there is something wrong; just how much is wrong he has yet to discover. For Jean, the sense of turmoil, sadness and isolation are becoming far more acute by the day. Even her husband cannot imagine quite how shaky her state has become.

### Adolescent blues?

Living in a hall of residence is a good start socially for any eighteen-year-old college student. Philip made friends with a lively bunch of students when he began his studies, some eighteen months ago. Just recently several of them have come to share a flat together, and they have managed to remain on good terms, sharing at some depth a great deal of their daily lives and experience. It is since moving into the flat that Philip has become a committed Christian, mainly through the love and influence of these Christian friends. It has clearly made quite an impact on Philip's own life and outlook, especially considering his background and the difficulties of his growing years.

Philip comes from a broken home. As far back as he can remember there have always been rows. His parents really did not get on. When Philip was ten, his mother left his father for another man. It made quite an impact on him at first. Emotionally, it was quite a blow for a young boy to cope with. Philip remembers crying himself to sleep night after night. It went on for months – until he made a decision. He made up his mind actively to hate and detest the man who had taken his mother away.

All that happened a long time ago, and Philip has put most of the thoughts of those days well behind him. It is true that an experience of that sort never fails to leave its mark; and probably for these reasons, Philip has developed into a sensitive and emotionally volatile sort of person. It is an aspect of himself that Philip prefers to hide, for he doesn't like others to see his sensitive side at all. He consciously covers all this up with an effective defence mechanism. He has learnt to protect his sensitive inner world with a friendly outer bravado, and sharp sense of humour, which has made him into an altogether popular and much liked personality. He is the sort of person it is fun to have around.

Philip's present gloominess is all the more striking. The fact of his sudden quietness, and apparently introspective attitudes has been an unexpected development for Philip's friends. They have not seen this side of him before. Some of them put it down to his recent broken romance. Such disappointments always take their toll. They were perhaps unaware that the relationship had been allowed to fizzle out. There was no dramatic end as such. Philip just seemed to lose interest. He was, in fact, relieved when Karen had called it a day. It had saved him the trouble.

'What's come over him? He's looking so tired and fed up.

He's hardly said a word to anyone in the last couple of days.'

Several of Philip's friends have been making such remarks about him. In fact, Philip has not got it in him to talk to any one at present; and that is part of the problem. He feels so uncommunicative. It is quite a struggle to put anything into words. He feels caught, trapped in a box. Neither is he sleeping well. He feels low, worried, really out of sorts. It is so unlike him. Every task is wearisome.

The seminar brought it all to a head. Philip is usually able to make a reasonably articulate contribution when called on by his tutor. On the odd occasions when he fails to prepare his material properly, like many bright students, he usually manages to bluff his way through with a combination of academic flair, and ready wit. This time, however, the prospect is unusually daunting. The inner fear is becoming paralysing. Just motivating himself to actually enter the seminar room is bad enough. He knows instinctively that he is not going to be able to cope. If he is called on to speak, everybody will know he is falling apart; he simply won't be able to string a whole sentence coherently together. His palms began to feel sticky.

As it happened, his tutor picked on him right at the end of the seminar. It should have been all right, as it was a relatively simple question, but Philip couldn't manage. He felt that unwelcome sense of panic and fear bubbling up inside. Making some mumbled excuse about not feeling well, a pain in the stomach, a sick feeling, Philip quickly left the room. He ran from the seminar room to the toilets. But he wasn't sick. There was no pain in the stomach. But he was feeling bad. Off colour. Not at all himself. When one of his friends found him a few minutes later, he was sobbing uncontrollably.

### Mid-life crisis?

Richard is a most successful business executive. His achievements are admired, and he works hard at his work, which he normally enjoys. Richard has a history of depression although he would not put it quite like that. He would describe it as one or two bouts of the blues; enough to make him feel gloomy and not himself, but nothing much more dramatic.

When Richard recently started waking far earlier in the morning than he does normally, his mind racing with thoughts and anxious concerns, a total inability to turn off and get back to sleep, Richard knew he was heading for trouble. It was bewildering. He was feeling slower all round. His memory wasn't as sharp as normal; and for someone in his line of business that is serious.

'Fancy not being able to remember telephone numbers, and feeling nervous about new clients.'

When Richard talked it over with his wife, she was accepting and reassuring. It was a relief to be honest with someone else about the way he felt. Rest, relaxation and some early nights is what they decided between themselves were the order of the day; hopefully, that would make a real difference.


## The way they are now


Anyone who has ever had any real experience of depression will be able to recognise some of the tell-tale signs in Jean, Philip and Richard.

For Jean the pressure is hotting up. The scrapes the children have got themselves into are certainly an element in Jean's growing sense of discomfort and dis-ease.

Philip is feeling tired and uncommunicative. Is it just adolescent blues? But why the overwhelming sense of panic in the seminar, and the need to run away?

Richard knows he has these periods of slowness from time to time. Like many successful businessmen he has an analytical mind. The wretched thing is he simply cannot account for what is happening to him. He has a very happy marriage, a lovely home, an excellent job. Normally he feels fulfilled and energetic. Is it a mid-life crisis? Why this exceptionally low patch? When he wakes up, night after night at 3 a.m., he sometimes wonders if he is going mad! It is an awful feeling; though by the time he gets up to make the early morning tea, he feels better and realises he is OK after all.

## Appearances can be deceiving

Sometimes those who are depressed reproach themselves deeply for not being able to climb out of the pit into which they have stumbled. Often those of deep Christian faith feel the resources of God ought to be sufficient to them. They pray, they confess their sins, they take hold of his promises. Why does God seem to be silent? How distressing that can be! It is even worse when some well-meaning, bright-eyed friend or acquaintance comes along, and with warmth and charm effectively suggests 'you snap out of it'. If only you could, you would have done so weeks ago!

As we saw in chapter one, the reasons we get depressed are complex. Sometimes it is possible to say, 'I am depressed because . . .'. Though even then what we think is causing us discomfort, and what actually is the cause, can be different. In relation to the three real-life studies – Jean, Philip and Richard – what can we say in respect of this?

Perhaps Jean's trouble is linked to the children's waywardness – maybe her present feelings are a complex reaction to the changes and traumas brought by her children's adolescence? Of course, this may not be the explanation. But if it is, is the cure going to be found that easily? Jean cannot withdraw from her situation, and if the problem itself won't go away – then what do you do?

Consider Philip. Is it a clear case of needing more early nights? You know how students burn the candle at both ends. Or perhaps it's a straight case of disappointment. Did his girlfriend have anything to do with it? And, of course, when you are at an age when your identity is making a further stage of development, everything that has given rise to the way you see yourself now is still around waiting to make itself felt if an opportunity presents itself.

Richard isn't content with the explanation that he seems to be prone to these periods of so-called depression. Everything has a cause. Apart from his business success, Richard is a well-known Christian leader. The problem for him during these times is that God seems to be so very far away. He knows, of course that the Lord is always near, but Richard feels a great sense of spiritual unreality. There must be a cause. More prayer, more giving, and more service doesn't seem to help either. So what is the cause? After all, if you know that, you can begin to deal with it; all Richard's training in business management has taught him the right-ness of this approach.

## A day at a time

That had been Angela's wise advice to Richard for coping over these weeks. They have been married for over twelve years, and Angela has grown used to managing when Richard is feeling a little on the low side. But if anything, despite Angela's welcome words of encouragement, Richard is slipping downwards. He dreads the thought of work, and is becoming particularly anxious about doing anything active in public, especially anything involving public speaking.

When he did manage to motivate himself to going into the office, Richard's secretary became immediately aware of the change in him and his unsettled frame of mind. Sometimes these things show themselves in unusual ways. It was when Richard seemed highly agitated at a couple of minor spelling mistakes in a batch of letters, that his secretary decided his holiday was well overdue. She was right in many ways; for up to just recently, Richard had been working all the hours that God gives with the greatest enthusiasm. Perhaps it was all catching up with him now. She had noticed that morning how his hand shook as he picked up his cup of coffee. Maybe he does need a proper rest.

It turned out to be a bad day. When Richard experienced the turmoil of presenting his company's latest product to the press, he decided it was time for action. He normally sails through such presentations, relishing the challenge and success. It was such a trial for him this time; not at all his usual experience.

When Richard told his doctor about his broken nights and his anxious thoughts and feelings, it certainly seemed to help. The doctor prescribed some tranquillisers, Richard slept a little better, but the drugs left him feeling washed out all day. He began to get more despondent; the treatment was not helping after all. Maybe Richard had not told the doctor the full story. As by now he was feeling in need of some spiritual direction, he sought alternative support. The minister at his church read the scriptures with him, offering him prayer and wise and sensitive questioning. Unexpectedly he also re-minded Richard of the physical element in the experience of mood. It was explained to Richard that there are times when certain symptoms suggest depression is best categorised as a physical illness rather than as a complex set of reactions to certain life events, or as a purely spiritual phenomenon. It was best not to prejudge the way of handling such needs, for different states require different handling.

## All shapes and sizes

Richard's minister friend was right. Depression takes several different forms, and comes in a variety of shapes and sizes. Fitting the right kind of help to the particular form of depression is as much an art as it is a science.

A surprising number of people slip up at this point, assuming what is right for one will be right for everybody. It is not the case, and it is as well to be informed about the variety of depressive conditions and elements in order to be better placed to arrive at an appropriate mode of action to help and overcome the illness. Some popular as well as scientific approaches do make the mistake of assuming their particular insight provides the *whole* truth. It is wiser to take on board a variety of insights which better account for the breadth of experience and observations made by many working professionally in this field, be they doctors, psychiatrists, pastoral counsellors, ministers, psychologists and others.

So we look in more detail at our three case studies, and attempt to unravel the kinds of depression involved. The different elements of depression will undoubtedly overlap, and depression rarely exists in a completely isolated form.

## Jean – reactive depression

Jean's experience with the three children has all the hallmarks of reactive depression. That catalogue of calamities was the touch which flipped the switch as far as Jean was concerned. The sad news about Tim and his girlfriend was really the major issue. But the pressure of coping emotionally with the other two as well, certainly didn't help matters. And maybe there was more to it than even that?

In discussing reactive depression, we should be clear that reactions of stress and depression are not the same. Stress involves the reaction of both the mind and body to change which produces the pressure commonly known as stress. The management of stress involves both an alteration to external factors producing the stress, as well as modifying inner attitudes, values and responses which go to make up the person's own individual physical and mental reaction.

In Jean's case there is clearly an element of stress involved. The pressures in her situation have wearied her mind and body, and her natural anxiety for her children contributes further to this weariness. All these reactions may well have precipitated her present depression of mood, but there are still more subtle forces at work. For depressive reactions, though often precipitated by present events, are informed by many other factors. These factors include the characteristics of personality, our hopes and fears, and those significant events, values and experiences which are drawn from a past whose influence lives on under the surface of our waking lives with continuing potency and vitality.

This double element of reaction appears to be present in Jean's experience. We all bring the baggage of our past into our present experience. Someone who has had a history of persistent chest trouble over the years is more likely to be more severely affected by a heavy chesty cold. This relationship of past to present works in depression as well. Past reactions such as pain, sadness, guilt, and anxiety can very easily be drawn into the present to continue to upset us; especially when there are precipitating pressures, which, like the chesty cold, exacerbate the underlying condition.

*Forgotten pains*

In reactive depression, there can often be this double reaction at work, involving reacting to the present, *and* to the past. An element of Jean's experience involved just this further dimension. Formative events of the past, whether remembered or forgotten, mould our outlook, attitudes, emotions and reactions. An issue or an event doesn't have to be constantly lurking around our waking conscious mind to continue to have an effect on us. When there are conflicts within us, especially at the unconscious level of our experience, there will still be much activity going on of which we are unaware.

*Feeling dreamy*

Sometimes our dreams give us a clue to this fact. Have you ever woken up in the night or even in the morning conscious of the fact that you've had a very unsettling dream? A very unsettled day may not help, but sometimes, a 'bad' dream may appear unheeded. Most of us have had dreams like this from time to time, even though we are not usually very good at remembering the details. The feelings seem to matter more than the facts, as dreams are very good at reflecting our emotions and the way we feel. More often than not the dreams appear rather fantasy-like, in that they take on a whole jumble of events which only loosely fit together. Where there is conflict the emotion is clear enough. It is a horrid anxious feeling, sometimes even panic. There are times when an actual situation about which we are bothered dominates our fitful sleep, our dreams, and our thoughts on waking. It shows there is a close tie-up between our conscious and unconscious minds, for which dreams form a kind of interface.

Jean dreamed for several nights that she was in a building which had caught fire. She was there with her young children. Each time she woke up feeling desperately anxious. Panic and dread were her dominant emotions. They were, quite naturally, directed at the welfare of her children. In fact there had been a time many years ago when Graham was a baby that he had been slightly burnt in what could have been a very terrible accident at home. Jean had always felt herself responsible, though when the gas blew up in Graham's face, he wasn't badly hurt, and it was caused by a manufacturing fault on their new cooker. Nonetheless, the fear of that event long past provided a powerful symbol for Jean's sleeping mind to express her present anxiety for the family's scrapes and muddle.

## The interpretation of dreams

What attitude should we have to our dreams? When Sigmund Freud published his major work, *The Interpretation of Dreams* in 1900, a massive step forward was taken in the understanding of the significance of the symbols and images of dreams. Classical psychoanalysts still use the basis of this approach as an important diagnostic tool where there is serious mental disturbance which is responsive to the complexities and time demands of psychoanalytic method. But for most people who are not seriously psychologically disturbed, our dreams should be left as dreams.

It is a matter of some debate as to the importance of dreams for normal everyday life. Despite the growing vogue for the self analysis of dreams, in general our dreams are not there to speak to us, they are simply our brains doing their sorting out process of all the information, sensations and ideas which have been taken in since our last period of fully restful sleep.

Sleep is very important to let our brains be active. The activity is different from that of the day, for in some senses our dreams are the junk shop of the mind. All the impressions of the day land up on a kind of pile, and as our minds do their sorting out, many odd things get thrown together and then processed. That is why when we happen to intrude by accident and get a peep into what our dreams are sorting through at any one moment, it can be an odd, disjointed experience!

It is important to our mental health that this sorting out process should be allowed to happen in our dreams. That is why sleep is so important. We often find that having slept on a problem we wake up with the solution the next morning! This is thanks to the constant tidying, sorting out and sifting process working through the night. For the ordinary, generally stable person, our dreams remind us of the regular processes of our unconscious world, where activity is going on all the time, sometimes involving issues we have not thought about for many a long year. When unsettled dreams recur, like Jean's referred to above, they provide clues both to the existence of an unsettled state, and perhaps to what is bothering us. Provided, that is, we have not fallen foul of cheese on toast eaten too late at night!

## Philip – psychological depression

There are clearly times when past events appear in some sense more powerfully significant than what is happening in the present. All this provides a clue to Philip's situation. The past seems to be standing up and taking its bow. It is often a way into finding out what is going on in these situations to ask oneself about the major crises or traumas, often involving change, which we have been through. For a boy of Philip's age, it must have been heart-rending to see his parents go through divorce.

Such an event must have had an affect on him one way or another. It could not fail to have done. What were his feelings at the time? What did the whole situation say to him? Is there, in fact, after all, a tie-up with what happened to his girlfriend? There does not have to be, but there has to be an explanation somewhere for his depression. The fact that he still cannot talk about his mother without feeling a combination of deep longing, pain and anger in an overwhelming way, is worth taking into consideration. Is Philip feeling rejected all over again, in a way which powerfully recalls the terrible pain of his parents parting? Is this a pain which no one let him express to another human being or enabled him to understand at the time, and is now making an unwelcome reappearance?

*The hand on the trigger*

What is it that triggers off a psychological depression? A psychological depression is certainly a form of reactive depression. The reactive elements are sometimes hidden beneath the conscious levels of our daily experience, but are nonetheless real for that. These depressive reactions have something to do with issues, perhaps unresolved, lurking beneath the surface.

An easy way into this is to think of those issues which cause us particular pain or discomfort in the present rather than the past. If something painful, sad or difficult happens to me, I am faced with the choice between a positive or negative reaction. Positively, even though it may take time and effort, I can accept the situation, aim to move on forward from that point, and be realistic and creative in my attitudes. Negatively, I can resist the issue, even deny it, refuse to accommodate to its challenge, and be overwhelmed by its hurt.

Let's be clear and fair. Many of us who are perfectly reasonable people react negatively sometimes, particularly when the scales are tipped against us. There is a painful relationship, my friend leaves me, being aggressively unpleasant and undermining as he or she goes. What is my reaction?

I feel undermined, hurt, rejected. Such is the awfulness of things, a whole catalogue of difficulties recently, that I become bitter, refusing to let go, refusing even to accept what has happened. An overwhelming sense of indignation and pain remains.

## Danger, keep out!

It is the negative reactions which are our greatest enemy. I could have reacted otherwise, even though my reactions were perfectly understandable under the circumstances. But where these experiences of pain or conflict go unresolved, and the longer they are allowed to go on like that, the deeper they get embedded in our personality and the more likely they are to want to throw stones at any situation in our daily experience which bears the slightest resemblance to the original situation. This is exactly the case with Philip. Many of his most painful childhood experiences remain unresolved, and hurt him still. He feels the sharpness of their attack so often, especially as he is understandably vulnerable to the emotional pain of rejection.

That stone throwing gives us the discomfort we normally associate with the psychological dimension of reactive depression. To resolve the problem you have to go for the cause, though sometimes when the issues have been forgotten or repressed, it is not always that simple to get to the issues immediately. It is almost as if there is a notice guarding the way which says, 'Danger, keep out!' There is a resistance to anyone getting near to what is fragile and painful, and it certainly doesn't want the light shone upon it.

A teacher in a local comprehensive school found great difficulty at the end of the school year. She was particularly popular with her classes, but she found herself unable to cope with words or gestures of appreciation. This became so intense that she would regularly become anxious and fretful at the approach of the last day of term. It became for her a regular cause of a mild depressive episode.

As a child she had come from a rather sombre, old fashioned, church-going family who never showed affection or warmth. She had grown up with a negative view of her own worth as a person, and a total inability to know how to react when others showed any form of love or esteem. Yet she was loving and caring in an almost exaggerated way; this was a legacy from her own childhood efforts to win approval from her cool-hearted and sour-faced parents.

She was helped by seeing that she had to face up to the facts of her own inner sensitivities, and not to let them rule over her. It cost her a great deal, but the freedom came when she opened herself up to the possibilities for change. For anyone to move forward from situations like these, we have to learn to beat our resistance, and do the necessary work to sort out those old injuries, remembered or forgotten. If we don't, in their perversity, they will try and beat us, and it is likely that they will succeed.

Of course, what we react to psychologically is not limited to hurts and conflicts, though these categories can have wide application. Questions of identity and self image are often part of the package, as are hopes and fears and related emotional concerns.

The simple point to grasp is we are our past, our present and our future. We carry around with us the baggage of our own past personal history, we have set directions for our lives, and the hopes and fears we have for our futures all form plenty of material for our present experience to bounce off when there is a suitable trigger. It just takes one suitably threatening issue or incident which corresponds to some deep sensitivity within to provide material for a psychological dimension of a reactive depression.

## Richard – endogenous depression

A clue to Richard's situation, is that there is nothing he or Angela are aware of that should be causing him particular concern, either now or in the past. He is normally a balanced person, although he does have these highly active spurts from time to time, and can be exhausting to be with. It is not 'abnormal' in one sense, though in another way it could point the finger. If we recall the hallmarks of endogenous depression described in chapter one, it would seem likely that Richard falls into this category. Medical treatment is available for those experiencing endogenous depression, and Richard should seek help from his doctor or a psychiatrist for specific treatment.

## The many shapes of misery

Everybody agrees that depression is a miserable thing to go through. It has many shapes and sometimes can be a simple short attack of the blues, lasting a day and then gone. Other times it is more prolonged and needs a special kind of attention. Don't forget that depression can be part of perfectly normal physical conditions and changes our bodies go through, as well as certain kinds of illnesses we may contract. Pre-menstrual tension, the change of life, growing up and growing old, briefly after the birth of a child. All these are expected times when some may experience depressive symptoms.

How we feel is a reaction to a wide variety of factors within, outside and beyond us. To help with depression the main question we have to ask is *what is going on*? We have to ascertain the full facts about ourselves, then we are one step further forward to getting towards dealing with the situation, and finding relief from suffering. Pause for a few moments, and think about the following questions and suggestions. They will help you to become more effectively in touch with what is going on in your life.

* Do any recent events account for how you are feeling now?
* Are you otherwise in good health, or is there some physical or medical element in your general condition which could be relevant?
* Have you experienced any significant loss just recently?
* Does some persistent thought trouble you?
* Do you have any recurring dreams?
* Have there been or are there pending any changes which are important to you?
* Draw a picture of how you see what is happening to you.
* Now explain the picture in words, as though to someone who knows very little about you.

Such questions and exercises should make you much more aware of what is going on in your life at the moment. You will need time and quiet to respond adequately. Some of your answers will give you clear pointers to the reasons for your struggles. Much of the unravelling will be done in later chapters. If your depression, or that of a friend, is persistent, failing to respond to sensible self help and care, then the best advice is take advice. No one will think you stupid – far from it. It is best to find out just what is going on without jumping to conclusions. So much can be done to help. But it is important to make sure you are treating what is wrong, and not what is simply imagined. Depression takes many forms, and wise and informed help is always preferable to promises of easy solutions.

Lord, I can talk to you, because you are always near. But in your kindness, please give me insight into my difficulties, so that I may discover the way ahead. Thank you, Father, for the value of human sharing. So please lead me to a compassionate friend with whom I can share my burden, and listen to my pain, and – like you – accept me as I am, while directing me to help and healing.

Part Two

# The Painful Past

# 3

# UNDERSTANDING YOUR PAST

How well do you know yourself? The deeper our self knowledge, and the more thorough our understanding of those life
events which have lent shape to our personalities, the better
equipped we will be, should pressure, pain and depression
engulf us.

## The things we forget

Most of us are aware of certain aspects of our history and
personality make-up better than other aspects. However
good our memory, it is surprising the things we forget.
Sometimes we forget because something is too painful to
remember. Other times life's busy-ness crowds out the
opportunity to work through our feelings when a significant
event takes place.

Helen, a lady in her mid-forties, the manageress of a busy
department in a High Street store, lost both her elderly
parents within four weeks of each other. She took time off
when her father died to help with the funeral arrangements,
and to be quiet and thoughtful in her loss. It so happened
that by the time her mother died unexpectedly and suddenly
a few weeks later, the store was just approaching its busy July
sale period. Though she would not have wished it this way, it
was in consequence as much as Helen could do to find time to
make the necessary arrangements, even with her husband's
caring help.

After the two funerals, naturally, Helen felt shattered.

Well meaning friends told her 'life must go on'. And so Helen threw herself into her work, unfortunately leaving herself neither space to grieve nor room for others to lend support. Her needy emotions were squashed. Two years later, Helen began to feel depressed. It was an uncharacteristic experience for her. She had always thought of herself as bright and carefree. But Helen's emotions were not going to go away.

It is a fact of our make-up. Emotions will always eventually insist on a hearing.

## The writing of history

So how well do you know yourself, in terms of the life events which have made the most significant impact on your personality, attitude, hopes and fears? The emotional side of our inner human personality is a much more sensitive creature than the perhaps more confident side we display to the outside world. The reason for those sensitivities has as much to do with our reactions to that which has been said or done to us, as to those spoken and acted out events themselves.

Before we can untangle any knots towards which our sensitive emotions may be directed, we all need to be more thoroughly aware of just what informs the shape of our personalities at these deeper levels of feeling. And to do that we have to begin with the writing of history.

When you go to see the doctor about your sore throat, he will always begin with a few questions. How long has this been going on? When did it first feel sore? He may ask you if you have had a cold. Perhaps he may feel your glands. He'll certainly look at your tongue and throat. In all this, the doctor is seeking to build up a clear picture of exactly what is wrong. Your actual state may be more complex than it appears on the surface. He needs to be sure he has the whole picture. And when the condition appears more serious, he will then be concerned to take a complete history. Everything of bearing will be asked for. It's the proper way to arrive at a thorough diagnosis and an appropriate approach to treatment.

## Life cycle

Our lives are always in progress. We never stand still. We are born, we are nurtured, we attend school. We work, we may marry and have children. We enter our middle years, we will then eventually retire and hopefully enjoy a grand old age. But the progress is often not altogether smooth. Crises and sadnesses may perplex us on the way. Sometimes we will pick ourselves up well, sometimes such crises will disable, even oppress us. It is not just the events themselves, our *attitudes* to the events may count just as much.

We are strengthened for emotional self management in the difficult times of life if we have a clear picture of our life history. The following exercise is designed to help you think and map out the most important events and reactions of your own life cycle.

Look first at the diagram of the life cycle and ask yourself what would be the expected crises (e.g. leaving home, the first job, unemployment, marriage, facing up to singleness etc.) revolving around the changing circumstances that anyone will be likely to face in these periods of life development?

By aiming to see the life cycle as a full picture, you will accomplish several things. You will become aware of the need for adaptation to a wide variety of changing circumstances in life. You will see the general pressure points present at a particular time of life, and so you will perceive the importance of the added weight of unexpected crises when they appear at these times. You will thus prepare yourself to analyse your own experience with greater accuracy. In addition, you will be more keenly aware of the needs of others when you perceive their particular crises in relation to their life story as a whole.

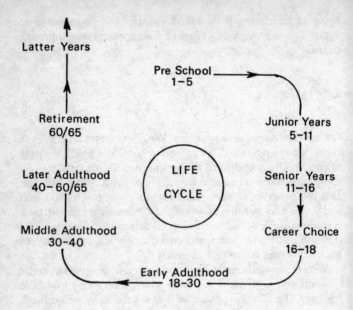

* Now plot your own life cycle history.
* Which life changes have affected you the most?
* What have been your most formative life experiences?
* What crises seem most important to you now as you remember them?
* What are your saddest and most unpleasant memories?
* Can you remember what it felt like to go through what you have described?
* Can you put those feelings into words?


It will help if you are able to put these thoughts about yourself onto paper. You'll not only have it for later reference, but it will help you to be more thorough in your analysis. Such an exercise may not be an easy experience to face, but the self knowledge it will release will be invaluable as you face up to the issues underlying your dis-ease. Finally, as a way of summarising your emotional discoveries about yourself, try this simple diagrammatic scheme of your emotional development.

Draw a straight line. The beginning of the line should represent your infancy, and the end of the line the present. The line therefore represents the progress of time. Now mark on the line any moments which stand out for you as being significant as painful emotional memories, and write underneath your age when these occurred. Now at a glance you have a profile of some of the more highly significant features of your life, with which you have either learnt to cope or maybe still provide certain challenges to you.

```
0 _____ x _ x _ x _____ x _____ x _____ 60
        14      18            33            44
```

**Life Cycle Linear Summary**

## The power of attitudes

Having opened up the book of the past for a greater scrutiny, it will be wise now to pause and evaluate an important dimension on the role the past can play in our present life experience. We all have a past. It is how we react to that past which will determine much of the depth and variety of the feelings and concerns of our inner emotional world. The past stays with us in some highly significant ways. Such, as we shall see, is the power of attitudes.

We must not slip into the mistake of wrongly portraying the past as some kind of bogey. Let's remember that for most people the past will always be the repository of many cherished memories. There are indeed many lovely things we are all glad to remember. Many value photo albums, family films and videos, and those little keepsakes and mementoes which we sometimes describe as having 'sentimental value'. All such are marvellous for reliving those really special moments which are so worth cherishing in life. This is, of course a right way of giving proper value to the past.

But all this has another side. We are complex emotional creatures, with the equal capacity for unhealthy attitudes as much as good and constructive ones. Have you noticed for instance how easily we can get stuck in the past, and let it exert the wrong kind of power over us?

Getting stuck in the past can involve a number of different reactions. We will begin here with three more common attitudes which may exist within us to events which are long since past. All three attitudes play a significant role when our inner selves become depressed. We could describe them in simple terms as nostalgia, inertia and guilt.

## Nostalgia – longing for the past

Nostalgia is often healthy and harmless. When the BBC ran a special and widely publicised series of classical jazz programmes on BBC radio just recently, they managed understandably to galvanise the interest and affection of many senior British citizens.

It wasn't just the special process to vastly improve the sound of the original 78s into modern sounding stereo, with all the cracks and hiss taken away, which occasioned all the interest. It appeared to be the reappearance of such famous names as Jelly Roll Morton, Duke Ellington, Fats Waller, Louis Armstrong, Benny Goodman, Red Nicholls and his Five Pennies, the Wash Board Rhythm Kings and the Dorsey Brothers, sounding as alive and vital as they had done years ago in their heyday, which caught the imagination so strongly. For many elderly listeners who were glued to their radios for the many weeks of the series, their glorious jazz past came alive again. It was pure nostalgia, and many admitted it. In fact, they were reliving their era.

But there is a nostalgia of a very different sort which is not nearly so healthy. Quite the opposite is the case. This is the nostalgia of the deep dominating internal longing. 'Oh that things could be as they used to be.' It's living for yesteryear, with your gaze set backwards. It is elevating the past into a golden age, and wishing that today and tomorrow could in fact be yesterday. This is the wrong kind of nostalgia, an unhealthy longing of spirit.

Look back at your life cycle analysis, and your linear summary.

* Can you perceive any points which spark off such a deep inner longing within you?
* What is it in your past which you long to relive?
* Why do you think you long so?
* How powerful and important do you estimate that longing to be?
* Note your findings down. They may provide some clues for later progress in these matters.

*Inertia – stuck in the past*

If nostalgia is a longing of spirit, then inertia is an attitude of mind. What exactly is inertia? It is that attitude of mind which says, 'Why should I change? I've always done it like this. Why do I need to change? Can't things stay as they are?'

Inertia literally means a state where you will not move. The fact is the world will move on, even if we do not want to move with it. Inertia can have far reaching consequences.

A glance at biblical history affords a fascinating insight as to the possible dangers of the inertia state.

How would it have been if Abraham had refused to move on from Ur of the Chaldees, and refused to follow God's leading to Canaan, the promised land? How would it have been if Moses had refused to move out from Egypt, and lead his people into freedom? If David had refused to become King of Israel? If Solomon had refused to build the Temple? Or if Jesus had refused to go to the cross? The world would be a very different place today. Inertia always has serious and far reaching implications.

Those implications can be just as easily seen in the personal realm as well. Take Sheila as an example.

It was a very sad situation, and the unbearable pain of it is only too recognisable. Sheila was a young mother. She lost her baby, Thomas, in a cot death when he was only two months old. Sheila and Phil were understandably deeply bereaved. After a while, Phil did his best to carry on with life; but Sheila found her days more difficult to cope with.

Four years later, Sheila still keeps Thomas's room in just the same way as it was the day he died. She lovingly, but painfully, attends to all the details of the house as though there were still a baby present. She finds herself still checking his room, and gazing at the empty cot several times a day. When her doctor asked her recently whether she had really accepted Thomas's death, she burst into floods of tears. She knew she hadn't. Sheila longs to have him back. She realises she is resistant to change, born of her unwillingness to accept the awful fact of little Thomas's passing.

Sheila will not move on and do as Phil has done and get involved in the present. We can understand her pain, but it is plain to see the danger which such inertia brings.

George is forty. He is bright and intelligent, but he does a low paid and undemanding job which frustrates him greatly. Drudgery it may be, but the great advantage of all this to George is the security it brings him.

Being a shy person, George finds it difficult to get to know new people easily. The job he is doing is one that relative youngsters tend to do for a couple of years, and then move on to higher things. George has known several young colleagues move on in just this way. Each time this happens, George gets more and more depressed. He knows he can't stay in the job forever. He knows he is stultified through lack of fulfilment and stimulation. But will he change? Will he do anything to help himself move on? The answer is no.

George is stuck in a situation of inertia, clinging to a fragile security, while his frustration shouts loudly at him to do something better. He is caught, and the fact he knows it just taunts him all the more. He is, as a result, becoming increasingly depressed. Strangely, he has little insight as to how to resolve the uncomfortable low state in which he now finds himself.

Many of us refuse to pay the price that adaptation to changing life circumstances requires. This is classical inertia. Biblical thinking indicates there are serious implications too at the spiritual dimension of our lives when inertia takes its hold.

The Bible's healthy emphasis is a balance. It involves the valuing of the past, the decision to live only in the present, and a focus on a responsible preparation for what the future holds. This is something the prophets of ancient Israel were quick to acknowledge. 'Forget the former things; do not dwell on the past. See I am doing a new thing!' (Isaiah 43:18). The historical situation behind those words is illuminating for us, because they are addressed to a people so full of inertia, they refuse to move forward with God.

This explains why the Lord's concluding words to them are so devastating. The fierceness of the outcome is to do precisely with the people's inertia, and their refusal to change and move forward. 'I will disgrace the dignitaries of your temple, and I will consign Jacob to destruction and Israel to scorn' (Isaiah 43:28).

This is a prophecy of the exile to Babylon, when the people of God were taken captive to a foreign land. The spiritual reason was largely their unwillingness to move forward with God, because they were stuck in the past. Inertia can affect not just individuals, but whole communities of people. Inertia has serious consequences. It always spells danger.

We should note at this point that anyone who is truly depressed will clearly suffer a slowing up process. It becomes difficult to motivate yourself. The thought of organising yourself for purposeful activity becomes a burden. These are the symptoms of the condition itself, where normal functions are depressed, and it is increasingly difficult to act as you do in your normal settled times.

But when you are your normal self, how then does inertia affect you? The question is important because the regular expressions and features of your personality will play a vital role in the characteristics of your depressed periods and how you handle them.

The negative sides of our normal selves are equally present in our low periods, as they are in our brighter moments. If we are grumpy, we may well get grumpier. If we are naturally weepy, we may get weepier. It is the same with inertia. In fact, there may be elements within some personalities where aspects of inertia in the normal times of life may provide a clue as to what is happening when depression sets in.

* Spare some moments to analyse any specific ways in which inertia affects your attitudes, feelings, actions or planning.

### Guilt – the past accuses

We all suffer from guilt in some way or other. Some people, however, are dominated by it. Guilt is experienced first of all as a feeling deep in the heart. Sometimes guilt is related to facts. Often it is a legacy from the past.

The experience of depression will often make the guilt feelings latent in our inner selves feel a great deal worse than normal. If there are guilt issues genuinely unresolved, then such issues are likely to take on far more threatening proportions than they have hitherto. The lowered self image, so characteristic of depressive periods, is aggravated by the guilty accusations of hurt and worried consciences.

What is actually going on in the guilty conscience to make us feel in these ways? The process is akin to punishing ourselves. Committed Christians above all should know that Christ has forgiven them, for the fact of guilt is the first and major issue addressed by the Christian gospel. 'My dear children, I write this to you so that you will not sin. But if anybody does sin, we have one who speaks to the Father in our defence – Jesus Christ the Righteous One. He is the atoning sacrifice for our sins, and not only for ours but also for the sins of the whole world' (1 John 2:1–2). But for those afflicted with guilt, whatever their outward profession, they know inwardly that assurances from whatever source are not good enough for them.

For Christians in this state, even the confident promises of the Bible will hardly penetrate the accusing core of their private world. As such, this makes their lot even more difficult to bear. To the burden of guilt is added an apparent lack of faith or unwillingness to believe in the promises of God. The tender Christian conscience feels even further disturbed for its plain and unallayed failures.

It is in truth a worrying and painful situation. The past stands up and accuses. It does so by day, and sometimes by night in dreams in which panic and fear play a significant role.

Yet the emotions do not remain silent. They are very much awake to what is going on. And what do the feelings say in response? 'You don't really like yourself, do you? Aren't you ashamed of yourself? Do you really think God can accept you the way you are? You're a fraud. Look what you have done. It is not really forgivable, is it?'

If you ever feel anything remotely like that, then you are not alone. Many have real problems with unresolved guilt. It is painful, and it can be crippling.

As we have seen the painful past assails us in a variety of ways. Its role in our inner lives can be powerfully active, exerting a terrifying, sometimes agonising hold upon our present attitudes and actions. We shall need to address ourselves next to how we can move on from this state of inward unhappiness, and learn to break the stranglehold the past exerts upon us.

# 4

# RESOLVING PAINFUL MEMORIES

Nostalgia, inertia and guilt need to be dealt with. The life cycle analysis we have already examined should give you a much clearer picture not only of your own life story, but also of your reactions to the past. People can get stuck in the past for other reasons such as bitterness and anger, though these are really the flip side of guilt – the unwillingness to forgive. Such emotions will be dealt with later. But for the moment we have to go to work on transforming our attitudes.

## Transforming attitudes

There are some other words of the Apostle Paul which are particularly helpful in this respect. 'One thing I do: Forgetting what is behind and straining towards what is ahead, I press on towards the goal to win the prize for which God has called me heavenwards in Christ Jesus' (Philippians 3:13, 14).

Paul is speaking to his readers on the danger of harking back. In his words we have a remarkably constructive approach in his positive attitude to the past. 'Forgetting what is behind.' 'Forgetting' (from the Greek *epilanthanomai*) is a particularly strong expression. It doesn't mean a kind of amnesia – forgetting all about the past. It is more definite than that. It means making a positive break with the past; a clear, firm and definite break.

## Memories

Often, if we have a particularly unpleasant experience, we will seek to deal with it by trying to forget. The man who secretly hid photos and memorabilia of his divorced wife in his son's garage was trying to do precisely that. The obsessional hiding of objects is sometimes an indication of a troubled memory desperately trying to erase the powerful impact of a painful, bygone truth. The trouble is, the greater the trauma, the more difficult that becomes. Our memories are largely efficient and reliable where the imprint has gone deep, and as such will stubbornly resist attempts to erase the painful facts which have been so carefully stored in our mind's retrieval system.

Difficult experiences are often reluctant to leave our memories. What happens is that we focus our energies in one particular way, the way of forgetting, and by so doing we fail to make any lasting progress with the issue. Whereas the kind of break with the past which these words of Paul have in mind, is far more to do with the exercise of the will.

## Accepting the unchangeable

Here is implied a conscious process of decision making. The decision involved often implies such basic approaches as plain acceptance of what has happened, or an agreement within not to argue any longer with what is plainly unchangeable.

A previously highly active sales executive in his midforties, a keen and successful amateur sportsman suffered a serious road accident. He was badly injured, and as a result he was unable to continue in many of his leisure time activities, particularly golf and swimming. This affected him greatly, and twelve months after the accident, he was bitter, sad and depressed. He longed to turn the clock back. He had tried to forget the horror of the lorry ploughing across the motorway at him. The memory of it tormented him in his dreams night after night.

He was eventually helped when he at last came to terms with the fact that he could not change the past, that the accident had happened, and that he must accept his present state of being. He became far more constructive in his attitude to his leisure time pursuits. In the end he did what he had always laughingly vowed he would not do until his retirement. He took up gardening. To his surprise, he found it increasingly enjoyable as his skills and patience developed. Today he enjoys his regular success in local flower shows. Significantly, his depression has lifted, and his nights are good. Gone is the understandable conflict with the past. The past he could not change, but could accept.

## The dynamic of Christ

Christians are greatly strengthened in their ability to break with the past if they dwell deeply and long on what Jesus Christ has accomplished by his life, death and resurrection. Jesus' life is a model of facing up to issues which were deeply painful for him.

His acceptance of the agonising inevitabilities of crucifixion with a will given over to God, provides one of the profoundest spurs to courageous living for any of his followers today. But supremely, his death on the cross, signifying forgiveness paid for, the power of the Holy Spirit to renew us day by day, and the assurance of the Heavenly Father's good purposes for us, both in this life and the next, provide for us the most powerful dynamics. Such dynamics enable us to put into practice the Bible's healthy balance. The balance which involves the valuing of the past, the decision to live only in the present, and a focus on a responsible preparation for what the future holds.

When the past exerts its hold with stubborn resistance, then it is essential to learn to actively rely on such dynamic truths. We must learn to fully acknowledge the only one who has ultimate power to deeply change the stranglehold with which the past can hold us, and release us from its grip. Jesus Christ can do that. He says that we shall know the truth and the truth shall set us free. He genuinely gives us hope and strength for the future, for he promises a quality of life in all the abundant richness which he brings.

*Breaking with the past*

How do we break with the past? Sometimes the approach is relatively simple. It is a matter of letting go. Sometimes letting go requires real faith. Faith is required because letting go can feel both risky and painful. We have to remember that one of the great secrets of faith is the actual faithfulness of Jesus to us when we trust him with the deepest concerns of our lives. He doesn't let us down, even when we feel very weak, and not up to coping with the situation. His strength is so often made perfect in weakness.

We can all understand people hanging onto the past and not wanting things to change. When you go through really dreadful experiences in life, you often grow weary. And it is in that weariness that you unconsciously train your thoughts to live only partly in the present. Far more, you tend to live with your memories, with the way things used to be. In some ways, it's a comfort. In other ways it can be a punishment. Old regrets, things which should have been disposed of years ago, hang around the closets of the mind, to dominate your attention, to undergird your values, to be your inner master. 'Do this. Don't do that.' The past dominates the present, and holds the future as much at bay as it can do.

## The guilty past

An old lady, near to death, confided that for years she had been tormented by the memory of having stolen something from her sister which had subsequently caused her sister some real disappointment. She kept it all a secret, and over the years she had not mentioned it to a soul. The memory of it became quite a burden to her.

When her sister died a few months before this lady's present illness, the old lady was overcome with grief. Her grief was as much characterised by a deep regret about what she had done all those years earlier, as for the actual loss of her elder sister. When she mentioned this to her Christian minister, she was clearly in a state of great turmoil. But by confessing it to God, and receiving the assurance of Jesus' forgiveness, she was able to experience that peace which passes all understanding.

For years she had suffered the cruel internal accusations of guilt. Guilt had stultified her relationships with others, and had caused her so much unhappiness. Now at peace, she died a few days later, serene and confident. It is sad and poignant to reflect that she could have known and enjoyed that same peace a great deal earlier in her life.

Where guilt exists in relation to a person now dead, the inner frustration and pain we feel has much to do with the impossibility of crossing the divide. 'I know that God forgives me, but my mother can't can she? She is not here any longer to be able to.' It is a worrisome, upsetting, and mystifying state. What indeed can be done?

In such a situation, it is wise to remember that the concerns of guilt are to do with the pain we have wittingly or unwittingly caused. But when a person has moved beyond the concerns of this world, such issues cease to matter to them. We might even say that if they were able to now see all the factors which gave rise to your words or behaviour, they would readily understand and would not withhold forgiveness.

It is possible to feel very bad about wrong thoughts, words or actions directed towards someone who has subsequently died. But when God says 'you are forgiven' that must be allowed to be enough. In God's goodness and kind purposes, whatever you did cannot have any ill effect on the person or persons now gone.

## Forgiving and forgetting

The Lord of the living and the dead, says, 'I will forgive their wickedness and will remember their sins no more' (Jeremiah 31:34). The divine decision not to remember our sins means our actual guilt will no longer be taken into account in God's thinking about us. If that is the case, we must teach ourselves to adopt a similar approach.

When God declares forgiveness, we ourselves must learn to stop taking our guilt into account any more. We must learn to agree with God that we are forgiven; that we are 'holy and blameless in his sight' (Ephesians 1:4); that the only right way of proceeding is increasingly to see ourselves in that light. Otherwise the sacrifice of Christ begins to count for nothing since it is not allowed to be powerful enough to penetrate to these sensitive areas of our bruised inner world. Ponder Paul's words in relation to this, 'If God is for us, who can be against us?' (Romans 8:31).

Paul's counsel, 'Forgetting what lies behind,' is a firm, strong decision to break with the past; leaving behind old longings, stifling attitudes, and crippling feelings of all kinds.

## Action required

Go back to the life cycle analysis in the previous chapter. In the light of your review of your own life story, ask yourself these questions.

* Is there some painful memory that causes me to hang on to the past?
* Am I hanging on in a way which is neither healthy nor builds my happiness?

Isn't it time to let go? It will involve both a decision and an understanding; for some of us can confuse valuing the past with holding on tenaciously to it.

## Back to the future

For some the future lies before us with many vistas of fear dominating its landscape. The future stands as a threat to present happiness and stability. Before we deal with the actual fear of the future, it will be as well to think about the ways of coping and planning for what lies ahead in normal everyday matters. Facing the future has much to do with embracing it, planning for it, and in particular with our attitudes to goals.

## Goal setting

In the early 1980s, the British entrepreneur, Alan Sugar, decided to make his electronics company, Amstrad, the single most successful computer company in Great Britain. Following his strategy, Amstrad grew from its small beginnings to become a highly successful multi-million-pound operation and number one household name. By the middle of the decade, they became the market leaders in their field. Amstrad, under Alan Sugar, is an example of highly effective goal setting.

When you have goals it means you give yourself direction. Companies have goals. Individuals should have goals. Christians especially should have goals. The Bible invented goal setting years ago. The Apostle Paul says 'and straining towards what is ahead, I press on toward the goal' (Philippians 3:13–14). It is not business management that dreamt up strategy. Paul himself was clearly goal-orientated. He was tremendously singleminded about his life and ministry, and as such it is an object lesson for us in forward planning.

## Learning from history

The best moments in Christian history are happily strewn with examples of ordinary men and women who set themselves goals and kept to them; from the historic heights of a Martin Luther with his passionate desire to reform the Western church, to many Russian Christians today who are determined to make the message of Christ known in a spiritually hostile environment. Find a life effectively lived at any level, and beneath the effectiveness you'll also discover a real sense of goal orientation, irrespective of whether it is understood in those terms or not. Many a politician, artist, musician, scientist or inventor will have taken a similarly dedicated approach to applying themselves, setting goals, and using all their energy to effect them as usefully as possible.

You could call it a one track mind. You could call it straightforward singlemindedness, if you prefer. Whatever you call it, it is exactly the same quality we notice about the Apostle Paul, 'One thing I do . . .'

## Learning from the Apostle

We see Paul's clear sense of direction, 'I press on towards the goal.' Paul's tremendous exertion of energy, '(I strain forward) to what is ahead.' And Paul's clear conviction of God's glory, '. . . to win the prize for which God has called me heavenwards in Christ Jesus.' For the approach to ways of coping and planning for what lies ahead in normal everyday matters, this singlemindedness is supreme.

* How singleminded are you in general?
* How singleminded are you in your commitment to Christ?
* What can you learn from Paul's direction, energy and conviction? 'I press on towards the goal. I strain toward what is ahead.'
* What can you learn from his concern above all for God's glory?

The promises of the Gospel of Jesus Christ mean we can be released from the stranglehold of the past, with its negative restricting goals. We are released in order to be able to serve Christ. The truth is that the reality of all this can be blunted when we get stuck in nostalgia, inertia or guilt. To value the past is a very different thing from getting stuck in it.

* Have you made a proper break with the past?
* Is there something you need to work on in relation to past events?
* Have you set yourself proper goals?

# 5

# CONFESSING AND FORGIVING

We have seen the distorted role the past can play in our lives. The need for a healthy attitude to such remembered, half remembered, and sometimes even forgotten experiences is clearly essential if we are to climb up out of the low and depressed moments into which such memories push us. But practically speaking, how can we approach a more healthy state? How can we break free?

## Know your story

A helping professional in such a situation will dig around to find out as full a picture of your life as possible. Sometimes resistance is discovered at just the points where significant facts or feelings exist. What would you not wish to tell someone in this situation? If there is something of that order, it may well be significant. It may cause you shame, embarrassment, or some other unpleasant feeling. It may be a trivial sounding fact or event, but the significance with which you invest it may well be the all important factor.

Are you normally in touch with the way you feel? Some of us repress emotions we cannot cope with, and consequently hold back emotionally on other areas as a result. If you have been thorough and honest to yourself in your life cycle analysis, try and be equally thorough and honest in your assessment of your resultant emotions too. Knowing your story in this way is indispensable if you are to press forward in the process of breaking free, for in the realm of the mind

and spirit the acknowledgement of need is the prelude to all
true healing.

## Releasing the emotion

'Are you angry?' The question was directed at a church
member who had undergone surgery which unfortunately
had gone badly wrong. It had meant a period of convalesc-
ence in which she had experienced terrible and prolonged
pain for which very little could be done. Her family, who
were all of quiet disposition, were kind enough, but felt
incapable of doing much to help in her misery. Her Christian
friends were also practically supportive, but Susan found
their confident assurances of good health to come, convinc-
ing but unconsoling.

Many months later after a really terrible period of disable-
ment, the physical discomfort at last over, she found herself
now bursting with mental pain and deep depression. The
repeated questioning about anger eventually released it. The
quiet, mild mannered, normally uncomplaining Irish girl
broke into a tirade of angry accusation. She sobbed, accused
and shouted, and became aware for the very first time of the
powerful depths of emotional energy in which her awful
experience had left her.

Anger faces us with several problems. If we bury it alive, it
will trouble us from within by its distorted protests at being
sent underground. If we give vent to its power, that alone is
not enough to bring us release. Active forgiveness, a letting
go of the issues which gave rise to our anger response is
necessary for our full release in both situations. Sometimes
we need help to recognise the causes of our anger. A sensitive
listener can often pick up those nuances to which we
ourselves have grown increasingly deaf. There are also times
when more professional help will be required, both to seek for
causes, and to assist in dealing with the anger.

Those who face traumatic experiences in life will know the

strong and sometimes irrational emotions such experiences generate. In bereavement, someone will feel they are just getting themselves together, when 'it all came over me again, like the engulfing of a great wave.' Many of us are fearful of the power of such waves of emotion. Societies differ in their ways of handling such feelings, especially in the initial stages of a traumatic event. This is especially so in differing approaches to mourning rituals. Whatever the cultural framework involved, periods of mourning nonetheless represent the recognition of the importance of emotional expression, and permission to express it.

Sometimes it is found by individuals that they have either not adequately recognised the weight of their emotional response at the time of a traumatic life experience, or they have not been granted permission to express it.

This withholding of permission may be on the part of family or friends who fail to recognise the emotional need of the sufferer, or who are simply unable to cope with it. It can also be the unwillingness of the person concerned to give vent to their feelings for a range of reasons and possible taboos. Such prohibitions may be a serious concern that the emotion will distort their sanity, that they would be unable to cope with their feelings, or that others might be repulsed by such an exhibition of what might be perceived as pure histrionics.

Such concerns, though common, need some straight talking. Emotion should not be buried alive. We are all wary of the emotionally self indulgent, and those who use emotion to manipulate; but the emotionally reticent do not fall into this category. If there is repressed emotion needing to be released, then it is important it finds a suitable way of expression.

The halving of problems by sharing is a true enough principle, especially when it comes to the expression of feelings in a caring and accepting atmosphere. 'It helps to talk about it.' Yes, it does. The most important first step is to admit the existence of hidden inner pain. The next stage is to face up to it, and make an agreement with yourself not to repress it any longer; but rather to address yourself to its expression and to its constructive management and resolution.

## Shedding the burden

Shirley surprised her friend by sending such a letter. But it had played on her mind for such a long time now that something needed to be done about it. Shirley's chance remark to a work colleague about a private matter relating to Jenny's health had caused Jenny some genuine hurt, and she told Shirley so in no uncertain terms.

It was quickly forgotten, by Jenny at least. In a practical sense, it made no apparent difference to their friendship. When Shirley moved from the area, she took her guilt with her, and it continued to play upon her mind. Then came the day she decided to do something about it. Out came the pen and paper, and five years after the event an apology note was written. It felt like the shedding of a burden.

Shirley ended her letter, 'I've learnt from my mistake. A confidence is a confidence. I should not have agreed to accept what you said to me in this way if I had not intended to respect your complete privacy on the matter. I am so very sorry for the hurt I caused you then. Please forgive me for it.' When Jenny's gracious forgiving letter arrived by return of post, it was as if the clouds had opened and the sun shone through.

It is clearly inappropriate to be running around apologising for every private thought that may be negatively directed against someone else. But saying sorry, and doing whatever we can to right a situation is good and constructive. This can, of course, get out of hand and become neurotic on its own terms. But many inner conflicts arise because of guilt burdens undealt with by the human dimension of repentance and penitence.

There is a deeper level still where burdens need to be shed.

It is to do with the way we relate to God, and how thoroughly we appropriate the assurance of forgiveness and acceptance offered in Christ.

## Life's playback

The Bible is clear we are accountable to God. When we die, and our lives are played back to us, we will see ourselves as we really have been in our many weaker moments. We will then have to agree that there is not only something wrong with us, but we are genuinely guilty before God.

But at the same time as this biblical awareness is presented to us, we are also offered a way out; a final lasting and complete solution to the problem of guilt and sin. This is really worth dwelling on. This lasting solution is all tied in with Jesus' death and resurrection. Jesus died, willingly and sacrificially by Roman crucifixion. He was and is God's own solution to the problem of guilt. 'For Christ died for sins once for all, the righteous for the unrighteous, to bring you to God' (1 Peter 3:18).

You may remember those words of the Apostle Paul in Romans where he says, 'The wages of sin is death' (Romans 6:23). Paul is summing up the biblical evidence that the whole disorientation of human life, physical and spiritual, is traced back to this moral dimension of sin. Decay leading to death, both physical and spiritual, is the consequence and outcome of sin.

## The way out

But Jesus' claim for himself is that he is God's unique way out. He taught that his death is a payment for our moral failures. That means when we stand before God at the judgement, if we have responded to Christ now, our account will be marked 'paid in full'. That is in essence what forgiveness is. It holds enormous significance for us, not only because we are informed in advance of what God's conclusion will be on judgement day, but as a consequence it possesses great psychological power as well.

'As far as the east is from the west, so far has [the Lord] removed our trangressions from us' (Psalm 103:12). 'You will tread our sins underfoot and hurl all our iniquities into the depths of the sea' (Micah 7:19). 'Though your sins are like scarlet, they shall be as white as snow; though they are red as crimson, they shall be like wool' (Isaiah 1:18). The Old Testament writers strained both imagery and language to express their rich confidence in the forgiving grace of God. This is a forgiveness which is valid for the whole of eternity.

Such confidence relies upon the unshakeable promises of God, and his merciful provision of forgiveness. 'The blood of Jesus . . . purifies us from all sin . . . If we confess our sins, he is faithful and just and will forgive us our sins and purify us from all unrighteousness . . . If anybody does sin, we have one who speaks to the Father in our defence – Jesus Christ, the Righteous One. He is the atoning sacrifice for our sins' (1 John 1:7, 9; 2:1, 2).

## Taking hold

How effectively we shed our guilt will depend to what extent we take hold of these promises, repent of our wrong ways, and believe our sins have been dealt with. It is a matter of letting go, and leaving our sins buried at the bottom of the sea.

Many folk with sensitive consciences will insist on dabbling with past wrongs. They will rake up their old failures and let them torment themselves again and again. Once more a decision to break with the past is essential. If God says they are done with, then so be it.

When a parent disciplines a child, there may well be tears

or even tantrums before there is a stifled 'Sorry, Daddy' and normal activity can be resumed. Many parents notice within a few minutes of a sharp word how their youngster is back, full of smiles and joy, the past put behind them. It seems a case of accepting that the parent's anger has come to an end. The relationship is restored. The slate is wiped clean. Life goes on.

We all need to learn from children in this respect. Jesus said, 'I tell you the truth, anyone who will not receive the kingdom of God like a little child will never enter it' (Luke 18:17). Children are far more accepting than adults. Learn from the child, and accept your forgiveness. What is past is past. The relationship with God is fully restored, and should be fully enjoyed.

* Is there something you need to confess to someone else?
* Have you fully taken hold of God's forgiveness?

## Dropping the charge

'I still feel bitter and angry. When my mother died, my family treated me so badly. They did me out of what was rightly mine. I've never forgiven them for it. What's more I never will.' The man in his mid-fifties was referring to something which happened over twenty years ago. Yet for years he had nursed his anger; refusing to let his prisoner go free, even after all this time.

When Jesus taught about prayer he used these telling words: 'Forgive us our debts, as we also have forgiven our debtors' (Matthew 6:12). Dropping the charge against others is a requirement for the dropping of the charge against ourselves. Our difficulty can be easily summarised in the words of the cheated middle-aged man already referred to. 'Why should I forgive? They are guilty. They have done nothing to earn my forgiveness.' And so they hadn't.

While we are right to want to see justice done, it is nonetheless true that we ourselves have not been treated justly. 'He does not treat us as our sins deserve' (Psalm 103:10). That realisation helps us to forgive others as we ourselves have been forgiven. The unforgiving heart is like a cancer. It eats into the system, eventually destroying our inner equilibrium, peace and joy.

As you come to the end of these chapters three to five, all of which concentrate on the painful past, pause for a few moments and ask this question.

* Who do I need to forgive?

Don't wait for them to make the first move. You have your supreme model and precedent in God's sending of his own son. 'While we were still sinners, Christ died for us' (Romans 5:8). If there is bitterness and anger within you, you need to learn to let go. If those emotions are directed towards persons living or dead, then take seriously Jesus' own call to the forgiveness of others. Without such forgiveness, the only one to be harmed will be you.

By dropping the charge, by forgiving in the same way as you have been forgiven, you'll be one step closer to freedom. Your inner energies will find new and more purposeful expression. You'll certainly experience far more peace and absence of emotional conflict. You'll begin to experience that liberty from the vice-like tyranny the painful memories of the past mercilessly exert on their unwary victims.

Lord, please help me to find a strength that I do not have of my natural self, the strength to forgive and let go of matters that have pained me for a long time. Thank you that I can do this as I realise how much I have been forgiven by you through your self sacrificing death. Lord Jesus, please help me through your Holy Spirit's power and grace.

Part Three

# The Painful Present

# 6

# BREAKING WITH THE PAST

When we are feeling at a low point, our minds will often wander to the byways of our past experience. We can find ourselves morbidly reliving our bygone sins and failures, angrily bemoaning the faults of others, and bitterly dwelling upon old injustices, hurts and sadnesses of all shapes and ills. Such is the nature of depression: what is past gets dragged uncomfortably into present awareness, to both pain and torment our fragile emotions.

But this is not the only way the past can seek to undermine our present happiness. The torments of forgotten inter-personal conflict, painful emotional experiences, and quenched primary needs can play a vital role in present discomfort.

## Playing an old tune

Paul and Heather have been married three years. They are both working. Paul is an assistant manager in a merchant bank; Heather has recently started a new job in a West End advertising agency. For some months Heather has been feeling low and out of sorts. She is not sleeping as well as she ought, and she finds herself irritable and tearful. Their relationship is suffering as a result. Heather feels unable to cope with any affection from Paul, which leaves Paul feeling increasingly hurt and rejected. At first, Paul put it all down to the stress of starting her new job. But the situation is getting worse rather than easing off. Paul is beginning to wonder whether he is the cause of all Heather's ills. But for Heather's part, she seems unable to put into words exactly what she is feeling. All she knows is that she senses insecurity within, and worrying question marks hang over her worth as a woman and as a person. Heather's self image is taking quite a plunge; she is not at all her normal self.

When Paul came home one evening tired and exhausted after a particularly difficult day, he completely failed to notice Heather had been to the hairdressers, and had put on a new skirt. All this was for Paul's benefit. Heather was making a real effort. Paul was simply not concentrating. The effect was traumatic. Heather felt increasingly disturbed within. After half an hour she began to sob and sob until the tears became torrents. To Paul's ears, her cries of, 'You don't love me, you don't love me!' sounded hurtful and mystifying. To Heather the deep disappointments of long years past were receiving a quiet but menacing playback under the surface of these present events. It was the same old forgotten tune. She knew she felt rejected. She also knew the thought was irrational under the circumstances. But there was no doubting the power of the feeling which would simply not go away.

## Early learning

It should come as no surprise to us that the past interfaces with the present in the manner that it does. Our lives are like the subtle interweavings of a complex novel. What happens on the very first pages and the unfolding of the early chapters will inevitably affect the shape, development and outcome of what comes after. Heather's childhood frustration with a father whom she adored, but who was consistently unable to give her quality time and attention has left its mark on her adult emotional needs and turmoil. But in the light of such fundamental influences, we also must say that our lives are not predetermined, as though we are locked into the inevitable constraints for good or ill of the impact of past experience. Nonetheless, thoughts, feelings, and actions are all subject to the moulding effect of what we have lived through.

The most important experiences are those which happen at the crucial points of change and development in our lives. Constrained we may be, but completely bound we are not. It is true to say that the vast majority of people can break free to a certain extent from the more negative of these influences. The grace of God is powerful in its workings on the weaker sides of our human nature, and we are indeed new creatures in Christ. But equally we have to say in relation to this that God does not normally change our basic personalities. He will change our inner motivations and their influence on our outward behaviour; but what has moulded us and what we are remains. On this side of eternity, God remakes what is already there.

Human personality is a wonderful, complex and unique reality. Any parent will testify to the fascination of observing the growth of the often very different characteristics in children of the same family from early on in their development. In children close in age, from the earliest days, tastes for food, or artistic and practical aptitudes may be completely different. This testifies powerfully to the stamp of uniqueness and individuality the Creator works into every person made in his image. But the fact of uniqueness does not prevent us being subject to powerful influences.

Our genetic inheritance not only constrains the colour of our eyes or our bone structure – personality characteristics are also involved. Early upbringing certainly teaches us good or bad table manners, but in addition it also bequeaths us a whole catalogue of learned emotional behaviour to draw on in later life, most of which has been unconsciously learned through parental modelling.

## The copy book process

Just as a child learns to write letters and words by copying
the shapes of the lines on paper made by a parent or teacher,
so is this copying process central to the world of emotional
and behavioural learning as well. A four-year-old may be
seen wagging her finger at her baby sister, when her mother's
back is turned. 'You're a very naughty girl. If you don't stop
that noise, I'll . . .' The child is mimicking her mother, just as
much as if she has hauled her daddy's jacket over her back
and is stumbling along in his size eleven shoes, trying to look
impressive!

The debit side of the copying process is that children are
like blotting paper – they soak up everything around, and
this means the good *and* the bad. So we shouldn't be surprised
that we have picked up some of the weaker aspects of our
parents' lives as well as the stronger aspects.

If our home was a place where everything was rather
serious, and spontaneous laughter, fun and hilarity tended
not to be approved, then children are likely to grow up
repressing this side of their instinctual life. If every minor
calamity was turned by one or other of the parents into an
emotional crisis, then that way of response will become a
learned coping mechanism. If parents were not very physical
with each other or their children, similarly this way of
expressing affection will be repressed. If sexual matters are
treated with embarrassment or swept under the carpet,
children may equally lose some of their ability to express
themselves naturally in a sexual way later on in life.

Christians are often worried about expressing their aggres-
sion. So it happens that the tight-lipped parent will cope with
strong negative emotion within by pushing it down hard and
refusing to speak lest his tongue should offend. This is
repression. Children of such a family will therefore learn to
repress their feelings too. Sulking, and withdrawal rather
than saying what you feel are the signs of this. The New
Testament, by contrast, does not shy away from emotional

issues, '"In your anger do not sin." Do not let the sun go down while you are still angry' (Ephesians 4:26). Children who do not learn these principles by example will not *fail* to learn, they will simply learn something else.

## Home learning

The balance of learning between parent and child is mainly to do with role models. So for a girl to become a woman, and later perhaps a mother, and for a boy to become a man, and then later perhaps a father, the parent of the same sex is the crucial model. We may well rebel in adolescence and adulthood, and say, 'I'll never be like my father (or mother) in that aspect of my life.' While it is possible to shed the aspects of learned emotional or practical behaviour about which we are conscious, that which we have learned unconsciously is more difficult to be rid of. So the person who says with vehemence 'I'll never be like my father . . .' may well say it with the same furrowed brow and tightened jaw muscles that he learned by example from his father over many years of silent modelling.

Physical behaviour and emotional characteristics, attitudes and responses are carried forward from one generation to another. Some of our distinctive emotional colour is the result of nature, most however is the result of nurture. Many of the powerful positive and negative reactions we discover within us date from these days of early learning.

Take some time now to reflect on the learning process you have undergone as a child in relation to your parents. You will gain much from thinking of your parents as models from whom you absorbed attitudes and responses, consciously and unconsciously.

To begin with, start by focusing in on specifics of which you will be easily aware. Then we will progress to what has been learned but not so clearly and consciously perceived.

* How did your parents cope with family conflict?
* Can you perceive anything in yourself which mirrors this way of coping?
* How did your parents express affection?
* Are there distinctively similar elements in your own way of expressing affection?

Now look at a more comprehensive picture of the influence of your parents upon you. Bear in mind the specific importance of the parent of your sex.

* Can you list those elements of your parents' *behaviour* which have most influenced you?
* Can you list those elements of your parents' *attitudes* which have most influenced you?
* Can you list those elements of your parents' *coping mechanisms* (e.g. the way they habitually coped with pain, sadness, joy, distress, fright etc.) which have most influenced you?
* Enter into the boxes below the three most important elements in each case which have most influence on your present life.

| 1 | 1 | 1 |
|---|---|---|
| 2 | 2 | 2 |
| 3 | 3 | 3 |
| BEHAVIOUR | ATTITUDES | COPING MECHANISMS |

Home learning exercise

## Understanding me

What is it that makes us distinctively what we are? There is no doubt that our upbringing lends an enormous input into our adult personalities, but we are in no sense mechanistic clones of our parents. We have certainly learned a great deal, yet every individual, heavily influenced though we are, is completely distinct and unique. So how can we gain insight into what makes us tick as personalities? There is no doubt that insight of this sort is immensely valuable for helping us face up to the difficult moments of our lives, and for helping us manage our reactions as effectively as possible.

We have already looked at what we have *learned*, now we will look at what we *are*. To help you dig beneath the surface, and get into the feel of describing to yourself exactly how and why you might react under certain circumstances, try this simple exercise in self description.

* Describe your real or imagined idea of a perfect day.
* Can you say why the elements you describe are so important to you?
* Now describe a really bad day.
* Can you say why the elements you describe are so repugnant to you?

If you have spent some time thinking through your thoughts on these two experiences, pleasurable and repugnant, you will be in touch with the vital relationship which exists between both your thoughts and feelings. You will have noted the relationship between your inner reactions and outward events. We will now seek to broaden that knowledge of your emotional awareness. For so doing gives much insight not only into how and when we are likely to react given a certain set of felt and actual circumstances, but also to modifying those reactions should their occurrence cause us emotional discomfort, inconvenience and pain.

## Hand on the trigger

'It's like a red rag to a bull.' 'That kind of comment makes me see red.' 'You just rub me up the wrong way.' These oft heard remarks make us aware of the importance of trigger experiences. Triggers are just like flipping a switch. We all have our own stock of them. They set us off on a chain reaction of felt emotions. Shout at one person, and they may feel unworthy, fearful or undermined. Show a kindness to another and they may feel embarrassed, indebted, or unable to accept the proffered action. Whatever the response there is likely to be some well-worn factor, hidden or not so hidden to occasion it. It works like a conditioned reflex. Given the right circumstances, a certain outcome is involved. As sure as the wagging of the tail when you give a dog a bone.

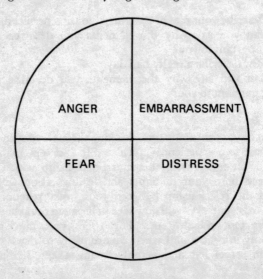

We are going to look at what effectively wags the tail given a number of different emotional responses. In the circle you will see four dynamic mood experiences. We are all likely to know their occurrence personally. How they are triggered is unique to each of us. So is their intensity.

* In each case, can you initially give one example of what triggers this emotional state for you. Then complete the following sentences:
    I feel angry when . . .
    I feel embarrassed when . . .
    I feel distressed when . . .
    I feel frightened when . . .
* Now in each case find a further two examples.
* Find a summary word or phrase for each trigger, and enter your findings in the towers below. Indicate the intensity of their emotional importance to you by placing the most threatening circumstances in the top box of the tower and the circumstances of diminishing power progressively lower on the scale, as the following example shows.

Heather described what sets her steaming inside and triggers her emotions of anger in this way. 'I feel angry when I am not appreciated, when I am taken for granted, especially when I am not listened to.'

| | |
|---|---|
| 1 | When ignored |
| 2 | When taken for granted |
| 3 | When under appreciated |
| ANGER | |

Trigger reactions example

* Make out your own personal inventory of what triggers your own negative emotional reactions in the same way as above.

| 1 | | 1 | |
|---|---|---|---|
| 2 | | 2 | |
| 3 | | 3 | |
| ANGER | | EMBARRASSMENT | |

| 1 | | 1 | |
|---|---|---|---|
| 2 | | 2 | |
| 3 | | 3 | |
| FEAR | | DISTRESS | |

Trigger reactions personal inventory

* Think of some other negative emotions you experience and account for them in a similar way, drawing the towers, and noting three triggers in descending order of personal importance.

You now have before you something of a self portrait. Here a picture is emerging of you in all your emotional uniqueness. Some of the elements you have described give you strength, some work against you and at times will cause you discomfort and distress.

What insight do you have into these feelings which you

find inside yourself? These truly are the real you. But how have such emotional responses come to be?

To get to the root of these upsetting emotions we have to involve ourselves in some careful analysis.

* Have a look again at your life cycle analysis. With the insight that gives you into the momentous times of your life, is there any event or events which has a bearing on the experience you have been describing?
* Look back to what you discovered from the home learning exercise. Think particularly of your relationship to those close to you in childhood and adolescence, have they in their personalities, attitudes or reactions any part to play in your present responses?
* With the insights you have already gained, try describing the most important characteristics and behaviour of your parents, or those closest to you in your early years, and ask specifically what impact any of those characteristics, behaviour, attitudes or reactions have made on you in your present responses.

## Where do we go from here?

Now it is a question of what you should do with the insights into your reactions and responses which you have gained from this careful analytical thinking you have done. It is one thing to say 'I'm like this because . . .'. It is another matter altogether to aim to use these insights to alter your behaviour and reactions.

Our responsibility for ourselves should help us to see that it is futile blaming our discomforts on someone or something else. Of course others have played their part, and how we came to be what we are and where we are is bound to contain some blacker moments in its history. We live neither in a perfect world nor among a perfect human race.

Just as we have our imperfections, so do those who have influenced us for good or for ill in our growing years and most formative experiences. Whatever has been is past and we cannot change it, and so there are only two possible responses. We either heap the blame for our discomforts away from ourselves, or we seek to use such insights to move forward and grow.

## Moving forward

Many people have a dominant negative emotion. This will be the discomforting feeling most often present when they are feeling out of sorts and generally low. It may be anger, fear, embarrassment, or distress. It could be another emotion altogether.

* What is your dominant negative emotion?
* How do you account for its importance in your emotional world?

Louise, a senior nursing officer in her mid-fifties, regarded herself as the worrying sort. She is a competent and warm-hearted personality, well-thought-of in the small local hospital in which she has worked for the last fourteen years. But although Louise has little difficulty in doing the work she knows so well, whenever there is a change in her routine, or a new or unexpected demand made of her, she finds herself going all to pieces inside. Worry, fear and panic are her unwelcome inner friends. For Louise, anxiety is her dominant emotion, and it not only discomforts her, but is also her primary emotional stumbling block in life.

When Louise sought help with this problem, a simple way of handling it came to light after some thinking and discussion of the sort we have just been attempting. She was all too readily aware that anxiety was her dominant emotion. There were two important stages which followed. The first was to gain *insight* into the origins of her feeling with the handle the insight gave her.

As a child, Louise was happy and positive. She was a bright child too, and loved reading and music, and was regarded rightly by her parents as certainly above average. When they moved house as a family, because of her father's work with the bank, Louise regretted moving away from her friends, but a particularly strong memory for her was being sent off to her aunt and uncle's home for three nights while her parents effected the move of house.

Her parents had excellent motives for the idea. They considered it to be less traumatic for a six-year-old to be out of the way when a move was taking place. But for Louise it was more unsettling still to be out of the action. Just because she was advanced educationally did not mean she was advanced emotionally. Louise needed to see the house being emptied, and have the experience of moving in to the new house, as well as having the reassuring closeness of her parents' presence. It was not surprising that her aunt had to phone up the night of the removal, and ask her parents to come and collect her, so great was Louise's distress. Unfortunately, by that time the damage had been done. Louise felt emotionally abandoned.

Another element is that Louise's mother used to react to times of change in a rather unsettled manner. So for instance, in the house move, Louise remembers overhearing anxious conversations between her mother and father, expressing worry and over-concern about the outcome of small details which would probably not have bothered most people. Louise has picked up this trait herself. It is positive in that she finds herself often giving a great deal of time to fine detail, which is a plus in her job. On the other hand, she can equally find herself becoming neurotic about minutiae, especially when she is worrying about some change of circumstances which may be imminent.

Louise has brought together two elements from her life

history and her learning pattern. From her past she has come to associate a major life change as a threat to her emotional security, and all these years later still relives the vague emotional memory of her childhood 'abandonment'. From her mother's defective way of coping with change, Louise has learnt an anxiety syndrome which expresses itself in feelings of dread, and a coping reaction of a kind of perfectionism, with over-attention to the checking and rechecking of detail.

## Dealing with worry

Most of us worry some of the time. Some people worry most of the time. Louise was a worrier. She came to see why and when. Worry is a negative form of meditation. It is chewing something negative over and over in your mind, till it begins to torment you with its challenge and threat to your well-being. It is one thing to have a worrying thought, it is another thing altogether to actually worry about it.

When Louise saw her predisposition to worry about change, she began to be armed for the fight. It no longer surprised her that she began to feel that way. Neither did she need to listen to her feelings so seriously. They have spent many unhappy years telling Louise 'do this – don't do that. Hurry up and check that – make sure you don't miss anything . . .'

Louise was able to get to the point of understanding of why she reacts as she does, and that took her on to the path of action. She began to say 'no' to her dominant negative emotion. She did not repress her feelings. More to the point she opened them up to herself, in conversation with others, and in prayer to God. Just because she had learnt one way of response in these situations did not mean there was no other way of action. Someone who drives on the left hand side of the road, can just as easily learn to drive on the right.

Louise now deals with the worrying emotion as soon as it arrives. 'Is there anything which genuinely requires prudent action? If not, I will not give the thought house-room. I will not chew it over. I will not let myself meditate upon it. And the old feelings of insecurity, which stem from that early experience of what I interpreted as abandonment need to be ignored, because they do not correspond with the actual reality of my situation.'

## The way forward

You too can break with the past. If you have worked through the exercises in this chapter, with the self knowledge that you now have, will you seek to break free in a similar way?

In 2 Corinthians 5:17, Paul uses these striking words to express the powerful working of the effectual grace of God in our lives. 'If anyone is in Christ, he is a new creation; the old has gone, the new has come!'

This means that the stranglehold of the past has been broken. John Newton, the converted eighteenth-century slave trader once testified to the remarkable way in which God is able to move us forward in our lives, no matter what has formed, moulded or powerfully influenced our personality, motivations or behaviour. 'I am not what I ought to be. I am not what I would like to be. I am not what I hope to be. But I am not what I was. And by the grace of God I am what I am.'

It will undoubtedly be of value to examine for yourself those areas where you need to change and grow. Talking with others too will provide not only insight but a help of itself as emotion is released in the act of discussion. In the end however, it is only in a trusting encounter with the living God that the discomforting elements which inform the painful present can be dealt with and progress is possible.

The truth is that in Christ the past is done with. When Paul says 'the old has gone' he means not only the cancelling of the debt of sin, but as the context makes clear, there is a new dimension to our lives. The 'new' has come, and we are new creatures in Christ. This must mean we are able to put the past behind us with its negative restricting attitudes, emotions and motivations.

* Write down what you have learned about yourself from this chapter in summary form.
* Spend some time meditating on Paul's words from 2 Corinthians 5:17, asking yourself how these words apply to you personally in relation to your summary. 'If anyone is in Christ, he is a new creation; the old has gone, the new has come!'
* Now turn your thoughts into prayer, and pray consistently day by day that God will lead you forward and help you discover a growing freedom from all that ensnares you.

Heavenly Father thank you for all that has shaped me as a person, for my parents, and for all the formative experiences of my past. Now Lord I come to you as someone conscious that I am not all that I should be, but thankful for your grace to enable me to break with all that is negative and weakest in my past and the way it affects my inner world and its bearing on the painful present. Lord please teach me where I most need to change, and give me grace daily to come to you for strength and power to do so. For I ask it in Jesus' name. Amen

# 7

# FACING SUFFERING

The painful past, with its negative celebration of all our inner yesterdays, is not the only raw material for our depressive states. There is no doubt that present adversity can be just as significant in its role in contributing to depression. Present turmoil may exert a most upsetting effect on our mental and spiritual equilibrium. Such adversity can be as internalised as fear or dread of some imminent and unwelcome event, or as actual and painfully obvious as a serious illness, bereavement, loss of employment, or a grave disappointment of some kind.

The painful present is a central factor to be reckoned with in depression. All of us react in some way or other to such occurrences. Sometimes we will find ourselves nearing the point when something tells us from within that we cannot cope any longer with the situation in hand. It is then the alarm bells ring loudly.

## Does God care about suffering?

James, a young assembly line worker asked just that question. His factory had faced a massive cutback in the workforce thirteen months ago. James has been without a job since then. That in itself has been dispiriting enough. Now to add to his misery, his fiancée has ended their relationship, tired so she says of his moods and tempers. James is truly down in the dumps. It was just a casual conversation with a friend from his church, but James cannot see the connection between his faith and his fortunes. 'If there is a God who cares about suffering, then why doesn't he do something about my situation?'

Many will echo the sentiment of that question. It is indeed important to know what God's attitude is to our present ills, especially if we are people who are committed to following Jesus Christ; it is important to face up to the challenge.

## Where is God when it hurts?

What can be said about present suffering to help us when we have to travel that way ourselves? It is not only the pain of suffering, physical, emotional or both, which tends to be wearying and dispiriting. It is also the suspicion of the futility of the experience.

Perhaps God doesn't care, or he is incapable of doing anything about it. It is the sense of hopelessness which is most depressing of all. Christians are not immune from such feelings either. We all need help at these times. As our vision of God and his purposes is enlarged, so our perspective on present adversity becomes clearer and more manageable.

## Sobs, sniffles and smiles

The first, obvious, yet central point to make about suffering is that it is there. We cannot escape it, for we will all experience suffering in different ways at some point in our lives. Suffering is always painful and mystifying, and usually deeply disturbing as well.

People in all ages have experienced and reflected on suffering. The character, Job, in the Old Testament cried out, 'Man is born to trouble as the sparks fly upward.' The poet Thomas Gray wrote, 'All men alike are condemned to suffer.' O. Henry, the American writer, said, 'Life is made up of sobs, sniffles and smiles, with sniffles predominating.'

When you are under extreme pressure and you are suffering, you do tend to ask all kinds of questions; and in a sense being a Christian makes the need for answers even more deeply felt. This has been the case throughout the centuries. It was so right at the beginning of the history of the Christian Church. The New Testament teaching on suffering is there to equip us for this universal experience common to all who share in our fallen humanity.

The letter to the Hebrews is deeply aware of the problem of suffering. These Jewish Christians were no strangers to pain and pressure. They were facing some real difficulties, mainly to do with opposition and persecution. Some of them felt like giving up altogether. Such felt concerns have a universal relevance, and a ready application to so many sufferers today. The writer's purpose was to help them find out that God does care about suffering, and that he offers help in it.

These are some of the questions beneath the surface of the letter to the Hebrews which are important to us too as we think about the painful present. In their turmoil, the Hebrews were asking about fundamental issues. *Is God too distant to come to our aid? Is God powerful enough to be able to change us? Does God care enough to help us when we are actually going through the experience of suffering?* These questions about God's control, his strength, and his compassion are at the heart of the unknown writer's presentation of the centrality of Jesus Christ for our situation.

## Is God too distant to come to our aid?

What kind of a world do we live in? Our view of the way things are will undoubtedly affect our perception and expectations. Is God close at hand or is he far, far away, beyond the reach of ordinary people?

Yuri Gagarin, the famous Soviet cosmonaut, was born in

Smolensk in 1934. He died in a plane crash in 1968. He was famous, of course, for being the first man in space. He went completely round the earth in the Vostok Spaceship Satellite back in 1961. A fact which is a little less well known about Yuri Gagarin is something he said about God. It was recorded in the Russian newspaper Pravda on Gagarin's return from that historic flight.

Yuri Gagarin said he had carefully observed the world from his space craft, but from his observation window he had not seen God out there anywhere at all. With all confidence he declared that this proved the case – God does not and cannot exist!

This comment is not as superficial as it may sound to Christian ears. There are a significant number of people who do think of God as 'way out there'; as good as being lost in space; as distant or beyond. When Christians start thinking in this way about God, there is trouble up ahead. It is true that some people think of God as being so remote that in practical terms he might as well not exist at all; for if he is that remote, it will be impossible to make any contact with him.

If you ever feel that God is too distant to meet your needs, there are others like you. It is a very common feeling, and we all experience it for different reasons from time to time. However, what we perceive about God with our feelings, and what may be true of him in fact can be two very different conclusions, as we shall see.

If you had asked the Hebrew Christians with all their experience of opposition and adversity, if they thought that God was too distant to meet their needs, they undoubtedly would have answered in the affirmative. They were suffering. It was painful. They didn't believe they lived in a *random* universe. They didn't think the world was out of *control*. But they did think that God was too distant to matter, or at least to be contacted directly. He was too distant to act and come to their aid.

This is one of the reasons why there is so much talk of angels in the letter to the Hebrews. Some of these Christians had some strange ideas about God. They had worked out

that God was so distant he needed a message service to keep
the lines of communication open. That is where the angels
came in. We all have our strange theories about the ways of
God. It may sound strange to our ears, but this theory of
angels is exactly what the Hebrews had worked out to
account for how a distant God gets his message through.
Strange it may be, but it gives their wise pastor a fascinating
jumping off point to teach them, and us, about the God who
is truly in control.

Let's ask ourselves who is in charge of the world? Is it a
distant God, way out there, lost in space? Is it the angels,
these intangible spiritual beings? To whom is the world
subjected? Who is in control? Because when we suffer, we
want to know whether there is anyone who can alter what is
happening, and if there is any help that we can receive.
Otherwise we will end up not only dejected and perplexed,
but panicked by hopelessness and intimations of futility.

Who is in control? The answer of Hebrews is fascinating.
No, it is not the angels: 'It is not to angels that [God] has
subjected the world to come' (Hebrews 2:5). Man clearly is
not in control either: 'Yet at present we do not see everything
subject to him . . .' (Hebrews 2:8). Man isn't master of his
world. The point is almost obvious. But what is not necessarily obvious is the very next statement: 'We see Jesus, who
was made a little lower than the angels, now crowned with
glory and honour, because he suffered death' (Hebrews 2:9).

This is the heart of the writer's response to this whole
question of suffering. It is saying cosmically, globally,
nationally, personally, Jesus Christ is in control. God is not
at such a great distance he is prevented from aiding us in our
suffering. These words sum up the words of Jesus himself in
Matthew 28, verse 18: 'All authority in heaven and on earth
has been given to me.' As the writer to the Hebrews makes
clear, Jesus' authority is linked with the suffering he had to
face on the cross. All this is not easy to grasp. So we need to
look at some further dimensions to fill out the meaning of this
particularly strong affirmation about Jesus' role in suffering.
When we see the centrality of that role, it will help us take

our eyes off ourselves and see new and inspiring resources available to us.

## Is God strong enough to change us?

There is an important human dimension which we must consider as far as responsibility in the cause of suffering is concerned. Human selfishness, inhumanity and destructiveness is all part of the vital human factor. What can be done about the deadly sinfulness of man? We play such a large part in the pains of others, from personal cruelty to national and international conflict. Is God strong enough to change us? Is he strong enough to alter our human nature in such a way that something can be done about the human factor which is such an important part of the cause and misery of suffering?

How does Hebrews deal with such a central question? We are told that God chose to make his unique son perfect through the experience of suffering (Hebrews 2:10). It is quite a strange response. You might expect something more rough and ready. 'Yes God can end all human wickedness. He'll wave a magic wand and put a stop to it.' But that is not what is said. It goes far deeper. As far as Hebrews is concerned, it places this question in the whole vast perspective of biblical history.

In order to change things finally the truth is that someone is going to have to suffer. That is what sacrifice in Old Testament times had taught. Sin was so serious it had to be paid for. All those blood sacrifices looked forward to the coming of a redeemer, one who would suffer and pay the price needed to restore man to a living relationship with God. In common with the entire New Testament witness, the person chosen to suffer is Jesus Christ, God's own unique son.

Someone may well ask, if God is love, why should he want anyone to suffer, even Jesus? There is a biblical principle to do with the payment of a debt which will help us unravel this question.

Annie is a student. Not so long ago she found herself badly in debt through her misuse of her credit card. Not dismayed, she paid it all off with one cheque from her bank. But, unfortunately, she did not have enough money in her account to support the cheque she had drawn. A few days later there was a friendly letter from the bank manager. The bank was understanding, but of course, they could not simply write her debt off. Banks cannot say, 'It's OK, we don't mind. £700 doesn't matter.' There would be chaos if they did things like that.

Finally, Annie's father came to the rescue, and paid it off for her. She was very fortunate indeed, and is now a reformed character in financial matters. She has learnt her lesson; but if it had not been for her father it might have been very difficult indeed. When there are debts of this kind, as we all know, someone has to carry the can. You can't just blink and hope a debt will go away, for someone has to fork out in the end.

The New Testament is clear that Jesus' suffering and death is also to do with the payment of a debt which we cannot pay off for ourselves. With regard to suffering, his suffering and death teach us there is something worse than purely *physical* suffering to consider. What is even more serious is *spiritual* suffering. God doesn't want anyone to suffer the worst, final and lasting catastrophe. It is not his wish that we face a debt which we cannot pay – at the judgement. This is why he has chosen the only possible way out, to suffer in our place, to pay off the debt our sin has accrued.

God longs to restore us to knowledge and friendship with himself. The suffering and death of Jesus are right at the heart of the matter. Given human selfishness, inhumanity, and destructiveness, which are so often the root cause of suffering, this is what God is doing about the deadly sinfulness of man. Certainly God is strong enough to change us. The sacrifice of Jesus is a supreme act of love. The question is whether you are prepared to let God love you enough to change you.

* Is there something you are learning about yourself in your present experience of suffering, that you know God wants to change within you?

## The here and now

Life can sometimes be very very tough indeed, and being a Christian can from time to time mean being up against it in some very painful ways. So what about our actual experience of pain and suffering and sometimes overwhelming temptation?

*Does God care enough to help us when we are in the thick of it?*

In the midst of suffering and temptation, we all ask where we can find help which will really make the difference. Does God care enough about suffering to do anything about it when I'm actually going through it?

Most of us carry around with us a number of fears, lurking beneath the surface. Some fears we are aware of, others are there, but they only bob up to the surface when something happens to upset us. Some of us fear the prospect of suffering deeply. Because we fear we won't be able to cope, that suffering will crush our spirit, that it will destroy our life as we know it. These fears go very deep, and we shrink from the thought of it.

Of course suffering is not just limited to pain or loss. It also involves us, especially as Christians, in the area of temptation. Think about the price you pay, the struggle you experience, for resolving to do the right thing when you are in the midst of strong and sometimes overwhelming temptation. It can be quite a struggle.

What price, for instance, do you pay for remaining faithful in a troubled marriage, or for remaining sexually pure in relationships outside of marriage? For those Christians who face problems with homosexual feelings, how is it possible to deal effectively with temptation, and resist, in a way what you long for so much, but which in the end you know is wrong in God's sight – and sadly, if given in to, will eventually distort both your life and personality? All these are difficult and heartrending issues to resolve.

Those who struggle and suffer deeply with ill health, or the pains and increasing limitations brought about by old age, or those who have lost loved and deeply cherished friends and members of the family; all know the pain, confusion and sheer weariness of such difficulty in life. None of us is immune. We cannot escape suffering in some form or another.

Those first century Christians were right. If we are under pressure, and Jesus Christ has nothing to say to us about suffering, then let's give up and go back to whatever we came from. And yet we are given this strong affirmation. 'Because [Jesus] himself suffered when he was tempted, he is able to help those who are being tempted' (Hebrews 2:18). The question we must ask now is, how does Jesus help in suffering?

*Jesus shows it is possible to overcome*

Though Jesus lived perfectly, he was just as subject to the ordinary, everyday temptations and hurdles that we face, see Hebrews 2:17. Humanly he had no more reserves of strength than we have. Yet he overcame. Jesus is able to sympathise with our weaknesses. 'We have one who has been tempted in every way, just as we are – yet was without sin' (Hebrews 4:15).

We must guard against putting Jesus on a pedestal. There can be an unhealthy air of unreality when we do. A teenager said that Jesus' teaching on sexual discipline was not relevant today because Jesus was so pure and holy he was incapable of sin. Yet the Bible emphasises that humanly speaking, in a real sense, Jesus is just like you and me. He had no extra reserves of strength, but he did overcome. He shows it is possible to do it. Very often our problem is we don't think we can do it. But we can. We can in God's strength. God is not distant. His strength and power can be known now. The Bible teaches over and over again that you have to make a decision to believe it, and to put God's strength into practice. Jesus' example is meant to show us it is possible to overcome.

*Jesus shows us how to overcome*

In John 14:15 Jesus says, 'If you love me, you will obey what I command.' So whenever we are in a situation of pressure, we need to remember that obedience to God is, paradoxically, the way we find eventual freedom. That was Jesus' own way. 'He learned obedience from what he suffered' (Hebrews 5:8).

It takes some time before we learn that obedience, involving sometimes painful personal decisions and sacrifice, is actually the way of freedom. But if this was so for Jesus, it certainly will be so for us too. Jesus does show us how to overcome by obedience. It is not always a popular lesson. But it does work – every time.

Here's a spiritual health warning. Don't rely on your feelings. Feelings matter, but they are as variable as the weather, and they are a very unreliable guide to the way things are or should be. It is possible to wake up in the morning feeling glum and out of sorts. Attitudes can quickly become hardened, and quite soon nothing will be expected to go right with the day. Such is the power of our feelings to badly distort the actual reality in which we live. The important matter is to rely on what you know, and persuade yourself with all your strength to do it. Whatever you feel in the morning, get up and do everything in your power to make something positive of the day.

*Jesus matches his strength to ours*

John chapter 14, verse 15 needs to be taken together with verse 16. They make a unit. Jesus says 'If you love me you will obey what I command.' He then goes on to say, 'And I will ask the Father, and he will give you another Counsellor.'

That is a promise of strength, a promise of the Holy Spirit, the Counsellor. But do you see the balance? It is only when you are prepared to obey Jesus' commandments that you'll know the Spirit's strength, not the other way round. The same teenager who had found such difficulty with Jesus' teaching on sex, found a strength for self discipline which truly surprised her, once she had made up her mind to keep Jesus' commandments and had actually taken the step of putting them into practice. Jesus doesn't give the Spirit's power to disobedient Christians. You make the resolve to obey, and Jesus will match your strength with his, by the power of the Holy Spirit. 'Obey my commands, and I will ask the Father and he will give you another Counsellor.'

### Jesus gives reality to our praying

Because Hebrews reminds us Jesus has been tempted as we are, that knowledge can and should transform our prayer life. It means when we pray, we know this isn't an airy fairy God way out there, lost in space. This is a God who understands, because he has been through it himself, in the human experience of Jesus.

When we are facing suffering, however awful the experience itself, we can pray with confidence, because we know this extraordinary fact is true: God himself has suffered in Jesus. A clergyman who lost his son in a motor bike accident said how he found depths of comfort in his loss, identifying the agony which God the Father must have experienced in the death of the son of God. The death of Jesus certainly shows us that God knows what agony is like. He is going to understand when words fail me or my faith seems to crumple up under the strain. I can pray 'Lord, it's awful – just awful.' And he'll understand and he'll answer my prayer, because that's what he did when Jesus cried out on the cross 'My God, my God why have you forsaken me?' Make no mistake –

God understands what suffering means, and he is a God of complete compassion.

So if your picture of God in Jesus Christ hasn't taken in the fact that Jesus knows what it is like to be lonely; that he knows what it is like to be frustrated, to be angry; to be sexually tempted, in every possible way; then you have gaps in your understanding. If you don't see him like that, you haven't yet begun to grasp the humanity of Jesus. Dwelling on Jesus' humanity is meant to give us strength and confidence in God, the confidence that he understands.

It is like those rare occasions when you find a friend who has been through just the same kind of failure or disappointment as you – and really identifies with you. It is the meeting of minds. There is real communication. Jesus gives to prayer that kind of realism. Such an awareness helps us to have more honesty about our real feelings when we pray.

The world is a painful place. But whatever the appearances, it is not finally out of control, and God is not too distant to come to our aid. Jesus has the final authority. We need to know that when we are up against it. It is not an impersonal universe. There is love in the person of Jesus right at the centre.

At the same time, we cannot be equipped for the struggles we face unless we have responded personally to Christ. Your dark side needs to be dealt with. God is strong enough to change us. But suffering is not going to finally come to an end unless your part in it and mine is dealt with. We need to be changed.

We might say that the question is not really whether God cares about suffering, but whether he cares enough about it to help us when we are actually facing suffering ourselves.

The answer of the Bible is that help is available, especially when we face suffering and temptation, if we will be motivated by Jesus' example, showing that it is possible to overcome. Obedience is the way forward. God's strength in the Holy Spirit is matched to ours when we agree to co-operate with God. We have to learn to be realistic and

honest in prayer, for Jesus does understand what we are
going through. He has been through suffering too.

* Do you need to let yourself have a bigger picture of God in
  the human and divine person of Jesus?
* Do you need to take obedience more seriously?
* Do you need to seek God's help, and not insist on going it
  alone?

There is One who is both master of the universe, and
humanly has been made just like us in every way. If you trust
him with all your heart, he promises – he will never let you
down.

Part Four

# The Troubled Spirit

# 8

# SPIRITUAL RESPONSES

The World Health Organisation estimates that something like 100 million people in the world as a whole are depressed at any one time. Though not referring to the experience of debilitating depression, a recent study in Britain has shown that 90 per cent of the British population functions below normal levels of liveliness with a corresponding loss of sparkle. But the really telling figure from the British survey shows that 8.5 million people, that is 15 per cent of the total British population today, have the quality of their lives seriously affected by periods of depression.

Those figures imply that by the years of adulthood, most people do know something of depression in their own lives or of someone close or near to them. As we have discovered already, there are different depths and types of depression, and indeed different reasons for depression. But the prevalence of depression in the population as a whole shows that no group is immune, no matter what may be their beliefs, lifestyle, activity, profession or even diet.

It may sometimes come as a surprise to active, committed Christians to find that a friend, a member of the family, or even their selves are prone to depressive episodes and a deep attack of the blues. There may even be denial or unwillingness to accept that depression can strike in such a manner. Unfortunately to deny a problem does not make it go away. We therefore need to ask if there is a specifically spiritual response to the experience of depression, with biblical resources available to us for dealing with it.

## Singing the blues

There are, of course, many examples of those who knew the experience of depression in the Bible. Elijah, Saul, Job, Jeremiah, possibly the Apostle Paul, and even Jesus himself in the garden of Gethsemane, are some of the most notable. There is, however, one specific and considered biblical response which is outstanding for its depth of insight and spiritual wisdom in coping with one aspect of the problem.

This response is contained in Psalms 42 and 43. It describes the agony of the experience and suggests a way forward for coping and overcoming in one particular kind of depression common to Christians. The two psalms are grouped together as one in many early Hebrew manuscripts, as the sense flows from the one to the other. In them the psalmist sings the blues in a real sense, re-enacting his inner pain and bewilderment at the events which have overtaken him.

## Inner dryness

> As the deer pants for streams of water,
> so my soul pants for you, O God.
> My soul thirsts for God, for the living God.
> When can I go and meet with God?
> My tears have been my food day and night,
> while men say to me all day long,
> 'Where is your God?'
> These things I remember as I pour out my soul:
> how I used to go with the multitude,
> leading the procession to the house of God,
> with shouts of joy and thanksgiving
> among the festive throng.
> Why are you downcast, O my soul?
> Why so disturbed within me?

> Put your hope in God,
> for I will yet praise him,
> my Saviour and my God. [Psalm 42:1-5]

It is very important for us as we read these words, to hear and feel the humanness and struggle inherent in what this man is describing. His words vividly express the inner dryness so characteristic of depression.

The writer of these psalms was one of the leaders of the singing in the Temple in Jerusalem, a musician and spiritual leader. 'I used to go with the multitude, leading the procession to the house of God, with shouts of joy and thanksgiving among the festive throng' (Psalm 42:4). The use of the past tense ('I used to go') is deliberate. Something has happened to radically change the situation. This becomes clear when he says, 'I will remember you from the land of the Jordan' (Psalm 42:6). The writer is now nowhere near the Temple in Jerusalem. He is miles away, in the north, near the rising of the Jordan river. The geography is very significant. It shows he is not working away from home, or on holiday; it means he is in exile.

## The torment of exile

It is easy to use a word like exile, and miss the catastrophic feeling of what it must have been like. Imagine what could have happened in Europe if Hitler had won the war. Suppose that in your community all the men over eighteen had been forcibly deported. Think of what it would mean to be sent, against your will, to a foreign land to work in labour camps and factories, perhaps never even to return. You would be totally cut off, a complete change from everything you were used to. That would be an experience of exile. It is a very similar experience which lies behind the words of these two psalms.

The second book of Kings provides a hint as to the background to this psalm's historical setting. It talks about the sacking of Jerusalem by King Jehoash of the Northern

Kingdom. He captured King Amaziah of Judah, and it specifically says he plundered the Temple, and then took hostages with him back to Samaria (2 Kings 14:14).

Here is a Temple singer exiled in the North, and he is lamenting the fact: 'Why are you downcast, O my soul? Why so disturbed within me?' (Psalm 42:5). We must try and enter into the trauma of what he has been through.

### The price of loss

The word which sums up his situation is 'loss'. He has lost an enormous amount in different ways. The reason he is feeling wretched is because something wretched has happened to him.

We sometimes forget how important the familiar is to us. This man has lost the familiar world of Jerusalem and the Temple. All the places and the people he knew are far away. He has certainly lost his home and probably his possessions. He may well have lost loved ones in the uprising. He will have been witness to the horrifying events which violence, destruction and war inevitably bring. That will have made quite an impact on him too.

He has also, of course, lost his job. And when you lose your job, you don't just lose your pay, you lose friends and colleagues. You lose the familiar routine, and sense of fulfilment. You also lose, even more profoundly, some of the sense of worth and purpose and esteem, which employment brings. And though this man has not lost his faith, he is by his very situation, cut off from the encouragement, the warmth and joy of others worshipping in freedom. We could say that, spiritually he has lost his sparkle. All this lies behind the sense of inner dryness described in Psalm 42.

### The thirst of the soul

That dryness is graphically described. 'As the deer pants for streams of water, so my soul pants for you, O God. My soul thirsts for God, for the living God. When can I go and meet with God?' (Psalm 42:1-2). Try and get a picture in your mind's eye, of a wild animal desperate to find water. The picture of the deer panting for streams of water is a picture of drought. What does the image suggest to us? The psalmist is not just thirsty, he is parched.

The psalmist goes on to say that once he was nourished with joy and thanksgiving, but now, 'tears have been my food day and night' (Psalm 42:3). What is more, he finds himself deeply troubled by what other people think about him in this state. 'Men say to me all day long, "Where is your God?"' (Psalm 42:3). He is worried about himself, worried what other people think, worried about his witness to others, maybe worried that he is letting the side down. The fact is, despite his aspirations, he appears to be able to do little to help himself climb out of the trough.

Then he looks back to what he has lost. Here's the sense of nostalgia beginning to emerge. 'These things I remember as I pour out my soul' (Psalm 42:4). Can you sense the pained frustrated longing, which so many people experience when there have been large and unwelcome changes and losses in life? It is the feeling that says if only things could be as they used to be. 'I used to go with the multitude, leading the procession to the house of God, with shouts of joy and thanksgiving among the festive throng' (Psalm 42:4).

'Do you remember those days? They were tremendous times. Remember the things we did. The friendships, the joy of it. But it's all past now isn't it. It's all gone. Nothing left. If only you could turn back the clock. If only.'

It is not difficult to identify with that. The depression which is expressed so movingly is the psalmist's reaction to the extent and significance of what he has lost. It affects him spiritually, emotionally, and even physically.

It is this sense of inner weariness, the dryness of spirit, the pained inner turmoil, which is so characteristic of depression. And if you suffer from depression yourself, I hope you will persuade yourself to take some encouragement from this psalm.

*Depressives anonymous*

The very existence of this psalm shows that it is not wrong
nor unusual, as far as God is concerned, to get depressed.
People who get depressed often feel an exaggerated sense of
guilt and a much lowered sense of their own worth as a person.
The writer of this psalm experienced depression in such a
way, but it is also possible to see reasons for such a reaction.

The two psalms record a reaction to traumatic events in
the psalmist's life, possibly some time after they had happened. Bad experiences often take time to sink in. His felt
guilt, and his low self image were symptoms of the depression, not actually the truth about himself, only what he
was feeling. Feelings are never a reliable guide to the way
things really are, and especially not in depression.

This fact has implications for any sufferer today. You are
not an awful person if you are depressed, and you need not let
yourself feel guilty or be self deprecating because you seem
unable to do anything about it. Depression is not something
to be ashamed of or to hide. No failure is involved. This
psalm would not be in the Bible if God himself did not have
great love and compassion for those who suffer what Charles
Kingsley once called 'the mumps and measles of the soul'.

## Emotional depths

Some of the language used in this psalm is very evocative of
the depth of suffering depression brings. 'Deep calls to deep
in the roar of your waterfalls; all your waves and breakers
have swept over me' (Psalm 42:7).

Marine scientists have recently put a name to a frightening
phenomenon which has been known to seamen for many
hundreds of years. It is called the fifty year wave. The
statistics show that about every fifty years there is the
possibility of all the right conditions coming together to
produce a massive wave which can engulf a North Sea oil

platform, or a massive ocean going liner all in one go. The fifty year wave is thought to be the explanation for the mysterious disappearance of some very large ships at sea over the years.

The psalmist too is picturing the threatening nature of the sea. In his case, it is a picture of torment, probably associated with the torrents of a flooding river. He is saying there is not a storm that has not engulfed and overwhelmed him in this trauma of spirit he is facing.

'I say to God my Rock, "Why have you forgotten me?"' (Psalm 42:9). So the emotion is not only overwhelming it is deeply perplexing too. God seems to be at a distance, even inaccessible.

'My bones suffer mortal agony' (Psalm 42:10). All the pressure, pain and distress has made him physically ill.

'Why are you downcast, O my soul? Why so disturbed within me?' (Psalm 42:11, repeating verse 5). This speaks of pure emotional bewilderment. He cannot account for what is happening to him. Those who know depression will recognise how characteristic this is of true depression. Real depression plumbs the emotional depths. For those who have never experienced anything like this, such a psalm helps in understanding just what happens to the human spirit at these times.

## Spiritual resources

Psalm 43 deals with spiritual resources for overcoming depression. So let's be clear this is the kind of depression where there are clear reasons for the depressed feelings, and where the ability to reflect and rationalise are unimpaired. The psalmist is not suffering from endogenous depression which, as we have seen in chapter one, must receive medical treatment. What progress does the psalmist now show in his thinking?

Here is the breakthrough. 'Send forth your light and your

truth, let them guide me; let them bring me to your holy
mountain, to the place where you dwell' (Psalm 43:3). This
verse is the turning point. It is the moment when progress
begins in a spiritual sense for this exiled Temple singer.

The two psalms taken together are like a page from a diary
of spiritual experience. The part that we have is the portion
that records the day the diarist turned the corner, when his
tears began to turn to joy. We ought to be asking, what made
the difference?

There is no instant answer to depression. At the very end of
Psalm 43, when the refrain returns a third and final time,
though the mood is now far more confident, it is still a future
tense. 'I will yet praise him, my Saviour and my God'
(Psalm 43:5). The psalmist has, nonetheless, taken a big step
forward, from which it is possible to learn much.

*Looking back*

The most significant lesson to learn concerns the outlook and
perspective of the psalms. The whole of Psalm 42 is taken up
with the psalmist looking backwards. We can understand
that given his circumstances, but he was in danger of becoming stuck in the past. You remember his nostalgia
('These things I remember . . . how I used to [lead] the procession . . .' (Psalm 42:4) ). There's a fine line which separates
nostalgia from a morbid, backward looking regretfulness
for all that has been lost.

It is not wrong to enjoy the happiness of memories. Neither
is it wrong to be fully realistic about the pain some losses in
life bring us. But what the psalmist did, and what we have to
learn to do is to let go, and to move forward.

Do you see what happens in these words? 'Send forth your
light and your truth, let them guide me; let them bring me to
your holy mountain, to the place where you dwell' (Psalm
43:3). What was evidence of a mind preoccupied with the
past is transformed into a heart which is prepared to look to
the faithfulness of God for the future.

Many things could be said about a Christian response to

the experience of depression. Yet since this psalm is the only one to deal directly with the subject, we may rightly conclude that what is said here is certainly central and applicable to all who take seriously the spiritual dimension of their lives.

In order to understand the importance of the psalmist's words in Psalm 43 verse 3, remember that Psalm 42 is simply littered with great affirmations about the nature of God. He is the living God (Psalm 42:2). A personal saviour (Psalm 42:5). A God of constant love (Psalm 42:8). God the rock (Psalm 42:9). Truly, there is nothing wrong with the Temple singer's God, or his understanding of him. 'Why, therefore, are you cast down, O my soul? Why so disturbed within me?' You would think with all that knowledge of God he ought to be a little happier! He certainly knows a lot of theology.

*Looking forward*

Psalm 43 marks a crucial difference. The psalmist comes to realise that for all his confident assertions about the nature of God, he has to let go inwardly and deeply. Intellectually he knows that God holds the future in his hands, but he must actually let God take hold of his future. 'Send forth your light and your truth, let them guide me.' Those words summarise a maturity of spirit, and a willingness to let God take control, which is a very powerful dynamic in depression.

Whatever your need, you can learn from this psalm. It is not always easy truly to believe that God will see you through a painful experience or tragedy, an immense loss or disappointment. But he will, because of who he is, and for what he has done for us already in Jesus Christ.

It is one thing to simply acknowledge these things. There are always many who can say, 'Yes I know that about God, and I have heard it many times over.' But the true transformation begins when you move from knowing to trusting. This is the time when you actively make the decision to let go of the past, and genuinely trust God for what he will bring in the future.

Psalms 42 and 43 are the words from a diary of a spiritually

minded man who became depressed. They are words which
record the moment this troubled Temple singer began to
turn the corner of depression. And the same can be true for
anyone in similar need today. The progress comes when your
gaze moves from the past to the future, and you can say from
your heart, 'Send forth your light and your truth, let them
guide me'.

# 9

# BURNOUT

The experience of loss makes deep and wearisome demands on our inner world; but there are many other ways in which our spirits can be troubled. Exhaustion, or burnout as it is often known, is becoming increasingly common as the twentieth century hurtles us into the future, with all its demands, pressures and temptations. There is a vital link between burnout and depression. Though they are not the same, the physical exhaustion underlying burnout can heavily tip the scales, and either precipitate or worsen depression. Because the mind is sensitive to the body's well being, for sufferers of depression it is important to be warned and fore-armed against the significant dangers of such a process of self exhaustion.

Burnout can hit anybody. It is usually defined as a state of mental, physical and spiritual exhaustion. It can and does disable the nicest, ablest, and otherwise sensibly minded people. Not surprisingly, Christians are subject to burnout as much as anybody else. It is important to know how to prevent and overcome the problems associated with it.

The life history of Elijah is one of the most telling examples of such a problem. His lessons are remarkably contemporary in their application. Here you have the greatest prophet in the Old Testament. His achievements were considerable, and yet, Elijah suffered from burnout. Underneath, he was a man of ordinary human weakness and failings. And our aim is to learn from the highly realistic way the Bible deals with his example.

## The life and times of Elijah

The greatest event in Elijah's life was undoubtedly his
confrontation with the prophets of Baal on Mount Carmel. It
is impossible to understand Elijah's later plight without
taking the full impact of these events described in detail in
1 Kings 18 fully into account.

To stimulate our realisation of the impact of the most
important events of Elijah's experience, we'll imagine Elijah
in old age. He has the photograph album on his lap. The
grandchildren are around him, one on either side, the little
one on his knee. What do they see when he opens the album?

The first picture is of two undeniably ugly faces. They are
snarling into the camera. Obviously, they don't approve of
having their picture taken. Hardly the sort you'd like to meet
on a dark night.

'Who are they grandpa?'

'Ah, well,' says grandpa Elijah, 'that's King Ahab and
Queen Jezebel. They were King and Queen in Israel for the
best part of twenty-two years. Before you were born. They
were pretty nasty types. Jezebel was a really wicked woman,
and very powerful too. Ahab was just the worst king we've
ever had. Together, Ahab and Jezebel brought Israel to an
all time low spiritually.'

'Grandpa, what's that funny statue of a man? He doesn't
look very friendly.'

'That my boy is the cause of all the trouble. That's Baal.
Queen Jezebel called him Melqart. It's an idol. A false
fertility god. It comes from Tyre, like Jezebel. But the
dreadful thing was she used her influence to corrupt everybody's worship in Israel.'

'Were you corrupted grandpa?'

'No, but practically everybody else was. At one time I
thought I was the only faithful one left. That's why God
brought me in as his messenger. It was a real mess.'

'Grandpa, if God was cross about the Baal worship what
did he tell you to say?'

'He told me to announce a drought first of all. No more rain for three years. Trouble was King Ahab blamed me for it. It wasn't my idea, I was only saying what I was told. Didn't work anyway. We had the drought all right, but everybody just got angry. But there's a picture over the page. Have a look at that, because that's the really good bit.'

'Which picture is that grandpa? Do you mean the picture of the mountain?'

'That's right. That's Mount Carmel. Do you see that big crowd. There were 450 of them. And there's me. The one with the long beard. All on my own, standing by the home made altar. It's a pity it's in black and white, but you can still see those flames. It was a fantastic bonfire. And you know God set light to it himself.'

'What do you mean, grandpa?'

'I told you everybody got cross. They were even more cross by the end of that. You see it was a contest. That big crowd was made up of 450 prophets of the false god Baal. And what God had told me to say to them was this. If this so-called Baal god was so great, then surely he'd be able to supply a bit of fire for them. Who would answer first, Baal or the Lord? The first to answer would be acknowledged as the true God. They thought that was a great way of ending the argument. So I told them to build an altar, and put out something combustible, a few twigs and pieces of bark and so on, and we would see who was the true God. It would be the one that answered by fire.

'Have a look at that picture underneath. Can you see the Baal prophets dancing around looking worried and stupid? It's a pity you can't hear them. They were yelling at Baal to do something. "Louder," I said, "Shout louder! Perhaps he's busy. Maybe he's thinking. Away on business? Dozed off? Yes, probably dozed off!" Couldn't help myself, I'm afraid.

'Now go back to the picture with me in it. By the end of the day, the prophets of Baal had really had enough. And then of course the Lord showed his power, and really glorified himself. Down came the flames on the altar I had built. I can

almost feel the heat now. Don't forget we were in the middle
of a long drought. We were all hot enough to melt. Everything was burnt up within minutes. As I say, they were really
cross, but they certainly got the message. No doubt about
that.

'And then the rain came. Boy did it rain! God really
pushed home the message that he is Lord of heaven and
earth. It clouded over. Just a few drips at first. And then it
really poured. It was a deluge.

'See the photograph of me running? It was a seventeen-
mile marathon. Talk about exercise. When the rain came, I
ran all the way to Jezreel, in front of King Ahab's chariot.
Everyone could see that the Lord was the victor. It was
terrific. We were really on the winning side. Revival was
under way. Even Jezebel might get converted now. What a
time that was. Best days of my life.'

Those are the true, historical events of 1 Kings 18. What
Elijah did not tell the children is what happened next.

The Bible is not afraid to tell the full story about any of its
characters. The tremendously exhilarating and exciting
experience of Mount Carmel actually took its toll on Elijah.
In fact he suffered burnout. And 1 Kings 19 makes that very
clear.

## The characteristics of Elijah's exhaustion

Have you ever been so tired you can't get to sleep? Your head
can be so buzzing with thoughts, it takes you ages to nod off.
Then when you do, you sleep only fitfully, and when the
morning comes, it's a mammoth task to prise yourself out of
bed.

Imagine Elijah in a situation like that. All the excitement,
the spiritual energy, the marathon at the end of it. That is not
a recipe for a calming night's sleep. It's 8 o'clock in the
morning. The door bell goes. It's the postman. Special

delivery. Bleary eyed, Elijah opens the door. What's this? The envelope has the royal coat of arms.

'At last. My knighthood!'

It is not Elijah's knighthood at all. It is a letter from Queen Jezebel. 'May the gods deal with me, be it ever so severely, if by this time tomorrow I do not make your life like one of them' (1 Kings 19:2).

It's hardly a veiled threat. The Baal prophets have come to a sticky end. So will you, Elijah. You have twenty-four hours before you get your very own cloud and harp. It is clear that Jezebel was not at all impressed with the Mount Carmel contest after all. She certainly hasn't been converted.

What is Elijah's reaction? It's a blow. It is not what he expected. His confidence suddenly takes a plunge. 'Elijah was afraid and ran for his life' (1 Kings 19:3).

Jezebel had everyone in her grip. So it was no use going to the police, or anyone else for that matter. Why didn't he go to God? We'll come on to that in a moment. But we really should not blame Elijah for feeling afraid.

What happens next? Elijah is on a downward spiral. It is quite common to hear people talk about Elijah's depression. To be precise, he is not really depressed, he is exhausted, and dejected. And no one feels exactly cheerful when they are fast running out of fuel, and finding the whole of themselves inside and out coming to a complete halt.

'When he came to Beersheba in Judah, he left his servant there, while he himself went a day's journey into the desert' (1 Kings 19:3, 4). That must have been fairly exhausting in itself. How sensibly do you think this man looks after himself?

'He came to a broom tree, sat down under it and prayed that he might die. "I have had enough Lord," he said. "Take my life; I am no better than my ancestors." Then he lay down under the tree and fell asleep' (1 Kings 19:4–5).

When our daughter, Emily, was only two years old, we were having tea on a Saturday at about five o'clock in the afternoon. Emily was so exhausted from playing in the garden, she sat at the table, took one bite of her sandwich, and then literally fell asleep on top of it. In fact her little head flopped gently forward onto her plate. She was fast asleep.

Young children get exhausted, temporarily, quite easily; and they just as easily recover. But adults are different. Elijah's exhaustion was far more deep-seated and comprehensive. We need then to be more precise about his exhaustion, its characteristics and the reasons for it.

* Elijah had exerted a tremendous amount of physical, emotional and spiritual energy. He was excessively tired.
* He was working in a situation of conflict. Initially, it was the whole Baal worship issue. Now suddenly it is his own life which is under threat from Jezebel.
* Spiritually there has been a big turn round. Elijah has been caught off guard. He copes with Jezebel's threat, not by exercising faith and continuing to pray, as he had done on Mount Carmel, but by relying on his physical energy alone and he beats a hasty retreat into the desert. It appears that instead of praying, he runs.
* Elijah deprives himself of human friendship and encouragement. He leaves his servant at Beersheba, and goes off into the desert alone.
* Elijah becomes full of self pity and despair. He prays that he should die. 'Take my life [Lord]; I am no better than my ancestors' (1 Kings 19:4). Maybe he had set himself unrealistic standards. Perhaps he feels he has to prove himself or do better than his parents' or grandparents' generation. Whatever it is, he is very disillusioned with himself.
* It develops into a thoroughgoing self obsession. Even forty days later he is still showing characteristics of this obsession. He says this twice, once in verse 10, and again in verse 14: 'The Israelites have rejected your covenant, broken down your altars, and put your prophets to death with the sword. I am the only one left, and now they are trying to kill me too.'

Elijah was exhausted from long term over exertion. In consequence, he was anxious about personal conflict; spiritually self reliant; lacking in personal friendship and support; self pitying; despairing and disillusioned. Elijah had become self obsessed to the point where he thought that the whole future of Israel was in his hands.

## God's healing process

This healing process which God used to restore Elijah to health and well being contains many principles we can take hold of for ourselves.

### Rest and nourishment

Elijah 'lay down under the tree and fell asleep. All at once an angel touched him and said, "Get up and eat." He looked around, and there by his head was a cake of bread baked over hot coals, and a jar of water. He ate and drank, and then lay down again. The angel of the Lord came back a second time and touched him and said, "Get up and eat, for the journey is too much for you." So he got up and ate and drank. Strengthened by that food, he travelled for forty days and forty nights until he reached Horeb, the mountain of God' (1 Kings 19:5–8).

### A deeper relationship with God

Elijah may have been desperate, disillusioned, self pitying and obsessed, but God did not give up on him. More than that, he enabled him to understand deeper truths about God which would equip Elijah for a renewed lifestyle.

God speaks to Elijah (1 Kings 19:12). He speaks to him, not in the wind, not in the earthquake, not in the fire, but in a gentle whisper. This is a beautiful illustration of the God who deals gently with those in need. Maybe Elijah had thought you have to be a success to be loved by God. That is not so.

This God deals gently with those who fail. It was quite a lesson for Elijah then, it remains an important lesson today about a God who cares.

### The opportunity to express feelings

'Then a voice said to him, "What are you doing here Elijah?"' (1 Kings 19:9, 13). And each time Elijah pours out his soul.

### Manageable tasks

Exhausted he may have been, useless he was not. He needed something to boost his self worth. A manageable task. No more trotting up Mount Carmel for the time being; just the small but worthwhile task of anointing a couple of kings and a prophet, Hazael, Jehu, and Elisha (1 Kings 19:15–16). Not too stressful, but really quite useful.

### Human support

Elisha is the key to the fifth and last way in which the Lord restored the ailing Elijah. For God gave Elijah a friend, and a colleague, someone to share with.

These are the principles behind the healing process which God used to restore the stressed and burnt out Elijah. Rest and nourishment; a deeper relationship with God; the opportunity to express feelings; manageable tasks; a friend to share with. Such principles are equally applicable in both helping and preventing depression. Their neglect illustrates the dangers which exhaustion can exert on a mind predisposed to a depressive response.


## Burnout today

Every year in Britain, over 300,000 people die from heart and circulatory diseases. The kind of lifestyle which leads to exhaustion and burnout has become one of the biggest contributors to this killer disease. What can we do about the stresses and strains upon our system?

Here are five checkpoints to learn from. They are derived from the way God himself responded to a classic case of burnout. Christians are meant to learn from Elijah. Exhaustion and burnout are more prevalent in the twentieth century; but, as we have seen, it's been around for a very long time. It is all to do with violating basic life principles, mental, physical and spiritual. So here's a checklist to measure your own reaction by.

* The Lord gave Elijah adequate rest and nourishment. So are you pacing yourself, or are you overdoing things? Are you getting a proper rhythm between work, family and relaxation? Are you eating a proper healthy diet, with enough protein, carbohydrate, vitamins and minerals from a high fibre diet comprising fresh meat, fish, vegetables, pulses and fruit, to supply your daily needs? Are you supplementing the value of a healthy diet by taking enough exercise, and generally looking after yourself physically?
* The Lord brought Elijah into a deeper relationship with himself. So how are things spiritually with you? How is your relationship with God? What can you do to help your relationship with him grow and develop?
* God gave Elijah the opportunity to express his feelings. Do you need to acknowledge the turmoil inside you? Are you a person who hides your true feelings? Do you need to talk to someone? Just to hear yourself say things sometimes helps enormously. If you hide your feelings they will break out anyway in some form. Shut them in and they can do you harm. Elijah's example shows how important it is to be emotionally truthful.
* God gave Elijah manageable tasks. If you are at the stage where you are feeling everything is on top of you, you really must stop and take breath. You may have to ask

yourself whether you need to take some drastic action. Is your health, happiness and the stability of your family really worth risking for the sake of your job. Or, like Elijah seemed to think, are you really indispensable? You may well need a rest. You may need a change of job. You may need to take on something much more straightforward, and manageable, for a while. You are not a failure. Like Elijah, you need to follow God's best for you, as he directs.

* God gave Elijah someone to share with. Do you have someone with whom you can share? We all need friends who will listen to us and understand. It is equally important for us to give our friends the opportunities to say how they are getting on and what they are feeling.


Elijah was a man subject to human failing just like us. All of us need to look at the way we pace our lives. It is a health issue, and it's a spiritual issue. Many people who face burnout are those who simply will not listen to the warnings. That is part of the danger of burnout, the lifestyle becomes an obsession.

Remember when God spoke to Elijah, it wasn't in the wind or the earthquake or the fire. It was a gentle whisper. And if God has spoken, indeed whispered to you, about your lifestyle as you have read these words, it means he will deal gently with you. He cares about you, because he loves you. But don't delay in doing something about it, because your need to change could be urgent.

# 10

# COPING WITH DISCOURAGEMENT

Perhaps the most common form of depressive reaction is when life fails to go our way. To feel discouraged and fed up when circumstances are at their hardest will sometimes fuel a simple yet uncomfortable depressive moodiness. If however, the discouragements continue, then the weight of their discomfort can be the harbinger of a more serious depressive response. Discouragement affects our mind and spirit, and for the Christian there are elements of concern which will be recognised as affecting aspects of his relationship with God, especially when God seems distant and prayer unanswered.

What kind of person gets discouraged? It does seem that discouragement is common to everyone, for we all get discouraged from time to time, and the range of issues which discourage us is immense. Such discouragements range from the car which refuses to start in the morning, to more serious matters like marriage conflict, illness and the loss of loved ones.

We also have discouraging days as well. The alarm fails to go off. The toast falls onto the floor marmalade-side down. You get stuck in a traffic jam on the motorway. There is an argument with someone at work. When you eventually get back home, having had a puncture on the way, you find your daughter has spilt Ribena all over your bright new white jacket.

We all have our moments like that; but it's when the troubles go deeper and begin to pile up on us, that we find coping becomes more difficult. Our spirits sag; we become heavy-hearted; life becomes a genuine uphill struggle.

What does the Bible have to teach us in situations like this?

Are we simply meant to grin and bear it, perhaps wilt in the heat, or even go under with the pressure? Or is there an approach to coping with discouragement, which can make the load somewhat lighter and altogether more manageable and purposeful as well?

Paul's second letter to the Corinthians speaks to this issue with precise and moving relevance. There is no other letter of Paul which is more openly realistic about the difficulties he personally faced. What Paul says about those difficulties is particularly instructive on this topic.

## Realism about pressure

'Praise be to the God and Father of our Lord Jesus Christ, the Father of compassion and the God of all comfort, who comforts us in all our troubles, so that we can comfort those in any trouble with the comfort we ourselves have received from God' (2 Corinthians 1:3–4).

Many of the cults today make easy promises of a life free from pressure. 'Join us and all your problems will come to an end.' They all offer the same trouble free guarantee. It is certainly attractive as a claim to many people, but unfortunately it is not the truth.

What, then, do we make of the claims of Christianity? Christianity does come with many promises; but a trouble free guarantee is certainly not one of them; quite the opposite is the case. The Apostle Paul is highly realistic about this. The clue to Paul's outlook is in the phrase, God 'comforts us in all our troubles' (2 Corinthians 1:4).

Does this teach us that Christians should expect the experience of trouble? There is a clue to this question in the language Paul uses. The word translated 'trouble' is the Greek word *thlipsis*. It literally means 'pressure'. The Greek term is a strong word, implying an almost shattering pressure.

If you have ever made the mistake of leaving a bottle of

liquid in the freezer, you'll know how shattering the power of pressure can be. This is exactly what Paul is saying when he uses this word *thlipsis*. It is meant to illustrate the kind of pressure we can find shattering, if we allow it to build up.

Paul was no stranger to pressure himself, 'We do not want you to be uninformed, brothers, about the hardships we suffered in the province of Asia. We were under great pressure, far beyond our ability to endure, so that we despaired even of life. Indeed in our hearts we felt the sentence of death' (2 Corinthians 1:8–9).

No one knows specifically what Paul actually went through; but we can identify with how he describes the *intensity* of the experience. He speaks of the pressure he faced; of going beyond endurance; of despair. They obviously felt the end had come when he says, 'we felt the sentence of death.'

'We do not want you to be uninformed, brothers, about the hardships we suffered' (2 Corinthians 1:8). Why does Paul want to inform his Corinthian readers of his hardships?

The main reason is that Paul wants to scotch the idea of an easy-going Christianity. Of course Christians face discouragements, just as Paul did. But if the Gospel of Jesus Christ doesn't have anything to say to the immense practical pressures of our lives, then it is distinctly suspect as well as irrelevant.

What is more, if you're facing discouragement, you don't need to add to your difficulties by feeling you are a failure as a Christian. If the pressure is on, and you are not faring as well as you would like to, be encouraged by the Apostle Paul. He felt like giving up. He despaired too. Jesus warned that our lives would not be easy if we followed him. He said that in the world we would have trouble.

It is not, therefore, a failure of faith, if you feel like screaming or shouting or stomping around at the agony of it all. You do not need to feel guilty or a failure. Since Paul is so emphatically realistic about pressure, then so should we be. It is unrealism of a most destructive nature to attempt to spiritualise such discomfort away.

## Confidence in the face of pressure

Paul does not underplay the intensity of his difficulties. Yet at the same time there is a very real confidence, a kind of inner strength, which comes through his words. We should be asking, from where does he get that strength? His words make it clear, for it flows from his understanding of the nature of God.

Paul's description of God is full of depth of understanding. He describes him as 'the Father of compassion and the God of all comfort' (2 Corinthians 1:3). What does that say to us about the nature of God?

The word 'comfort' is the Greek word *paraklesis*. It means the one who comes alongside to bring comfort. It speaks of God's care for every aspect of human need. This thought is taken up by Psalm 23. 'Even though I walk through the valley of the shadow of death, I will fear no evil, for you are with me.' This is the confidence Christians can know. The care and the presence of God, even in the face of shattering pressure.

Often we find that Christians facing a terminal illness will grow greatly in confidence of this sort. That confidence is in the God and Father of our Lord Jesus Christ, the Father of compassion, and the God of all comfort, the one who comes alongside us to bring strength and comfort in times of need. James 4:8 puts it so simply. 'Come near to God and he will come near to you.' It applies no matter what your situation or need is. None of us will ever escape the pressures completely, but we can develop a confidence within them, a confidence in the God of all comfort.

## Purpose behind the pressure

We know we cannot escape discouragement, pain or suffering; but because God is behind our lives, because he is weaving all the threads of our lives together for our ultimate good (Romans 8:28), what we go through when we are up against it is in no way wasted or purposeless. Paul spells out just one aspect of God's purposes in these times of difficulties. God 'comforts us in all our troubles, so that we can comfort those in any trouble with the comfort we ourselves have received from God' (2 Corinthians 1:4).

Often someone with a similar experience can be such a strength to a person in need. This is often so in bereavement. Friends who understand can be such a help at times like this. With Christians, in particular, the help they bring is directly related to what they themselves have learnt from God through suffering. This is especially so in depression. Only someone who has been depressed can intimately identify with the struggle, pain and bewilderment which depression brings. It may be a cruel price to pay to be of help and support to someone else; yet such ability to help others shows the unique value of the experience of depression. For some there is added a deeper understanding of life which could be had in no other way.

This is the purpose behind the pressure which Paul is describing. 'God comforts us so that we can comfort others.' When life is getting you down, you have a choice. You can either roll yourself up in a ball and feel sorry for yourself; or you can make something good come out of what has happened to you, and go and help someone else. Someone, somewhere needs your support; because you know what it feels like, and you know how God can help.

## Prayer and pressure

'Indeed, in our hearts we felt the sentence of death. But this happened that we might not rely on ourselves but on God, who raises the dead' (2 Corinthians 1:9).

Abraham Lincoln said, 'I have often been driven to my knees in prayer, because I had nowhere else to go.' That is what Paul is saying. Real prayer is not shopping lists of requests; it is not mystical meditation, nor is it rattling through a liturgy. Real prayer is reliance on God; and sometimes we have to be driven to our knees with nowhere else to go, to teach us that we need to rely on him.

C. S. Lewis once wrote, 'God whispers to us in health and prosperity, but being hard of hearing, we fail to hear God's voice in both. Whereupon God turns up the amplifier by means of suffering. Then his voice booms.' This is both the experience and the understanding of Paul. 'This happened that we might not rely on ourselves but on God.'

In the relationship of prayer to pressure, Paul also speaks of the importance of prayer support for one other. 'On [God] we have set our hope that he will continue to deliver us, as you help us by your prayers. Then many will give thanks on our behalf for the gracious favour granted us in answer to the prayers of many' (2 Corinthians 1:10–11).

Christian caring must include space for the working of the Holy Spirit; for the pressures will build up, and there will be discouragements. Yet in the face of such pressures, Jesus Christ is always in control of our lives. He is looking to us to give him a central place that his Spirit may work in and through us. One of the ways we do that is when we pray for one another, for we are meant to bear one another's burdens.

If you are going through difficulties at the moment, and life is often an uphill struggle, then remember above all, the nature of God. He is the Father of compassion, and the God of all comfort. If you draw near to him, he will draw near to you. All this really isn't purposeless. You have so much to give to others. Remember that if you always dwell on yourself and your own troubles, you are depriving someone else of your help, making it worse for yourself in the end, because you are ignoring an important aspect of God's call upon your life.

Ask yourself: how much do you rely on God? It is not a question of church attendance, Bible reading, how much money you give away, active involvement in church life, or anything like that. How much do you actually rely on God himself? Because in your situation of discouragement, is God saying that he wants you to know a deeper and more real relationship with himself?

Paul knew the experience of almost shattering pressure. He was both realistic about the pressure and confident within it. The way he coped has much to do with his understanding of purpose. What was his conclusion in coping with his discouragements? 'This happened that we might not rely on ourselves, but on God.'

## Unanswered prayer

It is clear from the same letter, that Paul's difficulties never found easy or glib answers. His responses to situations of difficulty are all the more impressive for the fact that his experience of the grace of God was forged on the anvil of great personal discomfort and suffering. It is easy to imagine the great Apostle as somehow having a priority line to Heaven. Yet it is clear from Paul's correspondence that prayer involved great truth and joy, but also much struggle and heart searching.

Situations of deep mystification arise in the painful times of life when God's help seems inaccessible in certain ways, even though there is an inner desire to rely on God and do his will.

Suppose, for instance, you are facing a particularly difficult illness. You long for relief. The doctors have done their best; but there is little they can do. In all sincerity, you pray; and you rightly ask God for healing. Others come and pray with you; but unlike the experience of some of whom you have heard or read, in your case, nothing seems to happen. You ask yourself, 'What's going on? Am I a failure? Where is God, our great loving God, in all this?'

There are many varied examples of this awareness; not just illness, but unemployment, relationship problems, finances, finding a place to live; none perhaps more perplexing than the struggle with depression. They are all uphill struggles. Yet far from finding comfort and clear answers to our prayers, there are moments when God appears to go silent on us. We need to know from the Bible what it teaches at these difficult times, when we have to make sense of this sometimes confusing issue of unanswered prayer.

Later, in 2 Corinthians chapter 12, Paul talks about the whole issue of human weakness, and God's response to it. He quite specifically mentions his own experience of unanswered prayer. 'Three times I pleaded with the Lord to take it away from me' (2 Corinthians 12:8).

There were, in the church at Corinth, some highly influential Christian teachers. Paul calls them 'super-apostles' (2 Corinthians 11:5). He didn't think they were super at all. His term is derogatory; he means they were super spiritual. These teachers were claiming that suffering and discouragement all come to an end when you become a Christian, implying that wholeness and complete freedom from illness and pain is the right of every child of God now.

Paul views this as a potentially dangerous exaggeration. Of course, God answers prayer, including prayer for healing. But Paul is clear that we still live in a decaying world with decaying and declining human bodies. God is glorified when there are marvellous answers to prayer. Paul does not deny that; but he argues strongly that God's glory goes even deeper in the experience of human weakness. That is why he gives attention to unanswered prayer.

## Spirituality defended

You wouldn't think that Paul the Apostle would need to defend his spirituality to anyone; but he did. There had been a whispering campaign in Corinth. 'Don't listen to Paul. He hasn't got the victory. Some people don't think he's got the Spirit either. You're a failure Paul. You need to pray harder.

You need more faith. You need to be more spiritual.' People still say the same things today. So what is Paul's response?

Paul addresses the super-apostles on their own terms. He has already made it clear that actual reliance on God is the most important matter for the Christian. Now he speaks to them in the kind of spiritual language they will readily understand. He wants to get on the same wavelength; and that is why he uses the language of visions.

'I know a man in Christ who fourteen years ago was caught up to the third heaven. Whether it was in the body or out of the body I do not know – God knows. And I know that this man – whether in the body or apart from the body I do not know but God knows – was caught up to paradise. He heard inexpressible things, things that man is not permitted to tell. I will boast about a man like that, but I will not boast about myself, except about my weaknesses' (2 Corinthians 12:2–5).

Who is Paul speaking of? It's himself. He is the man caught up to the third heaven. If you know Paul's letters well, you'll know how down to earth he normally is. He does not usually go in for heady spiritual experiences. So why here?

He is describing a real experience; a special visionary spiritual awareness and encounter with God. Some people have these experiences, and most people don't. Yet Paul did; and he speaks at first as though it were someone else. This is because he does not want anyone to think highly of him for the wrong reasons. It is God who gives such experiences, and the glory belongs to him.

Paul is saying this to the super-apostles: 'You may emphasise the spiritually high moments. I'm not denigrating that. I've had my moments too – so don't write me off just yet. Of course God can do anything. But I tell you the way God is really glorified is not when we are strong, but when we are weak.' And that is how he introduces his thoughts on unanswered prayer. Paul defends his spirituality and his spiritual experience as being real and authentic, because his suffering has nothing to do with being a sub-standard Christian.

## Suffering described

'To keep me from becoming conceited because of these
surpassingly great revelations, there was given me a thorn in
my flesh, a messenger of Satan, to torment me' (2 Corinthians
12:7).

The thorn in the flesh is a very famous phrase, but what
does it mean? If you like gardening, especially if you grow
roses, you'll know all about thorns in the flesh. Some of the
bushy shrub roses have particularly sharp little thorns. You
need nice thick rubberised gloves to protect you. Yet a thorn
in the flesh is not a serious wound at all, you hardly need an
elastoplast to deal with it.

You may be interested to learn that Paul didn't have a
thorn in the flesh at all. The Greek word *skolops* which is
traditionally translated as 'thorn' really means 'stake'. It is
the word used of the stake upon which they impaled crimi-
nals in Paul's time. He is not talking about a tiny little thorn;
he is talking about a stake painfully impaled in his own body.
His expression a 'stake in the flesh' is no finger prick. It
describes a real experience of suffering.

What was Paul suffering? Do we have any clues? In a way,
there is not much point in trying to work out what Paul was
describing in specific terms. There are many theories, and
they are as numerous as they are specious.

Calvin thought Paul's thorn or stake was overwhelming
temptation. Tertullian and Jerome thought it was dreadful
migraine-like headaches. Roman Catholic commentators
think it was all to do with sex. Others say it could have been
the virulent malaria so common in the Eastern Mediter-
ranean. It could have something to do with his experience of
opposition and persecution. It perhaps had something to do
with his eyesight.

The eyesight theory may have something to commend it.
Paul was blinded on the Damascus road for a period of
time. He always used an amanuensis for his letters. At
the end of Galatians, when he writes his own greeting, he

says, 'See what large letters I use as I write to you' (Galatians 6:11).

It really doesn't matter what it was he was suffering from. It is the intensity of the experience which counts. It is not a little thorn. It is a great big stake. He describes this infirmity as 'a messenger of Satan, to torment me.'

It is important also to note how once again Paul makes sense of his suffering. He can see purpose in it. He says all this happened to him in order 'to keep me from becoming conceited' (2 Corinthians 12:7).

It is very instructive to see how Paul made sense of his suffering. We need to understand that this conclusion is the result of mature reflection. It is highly unlikely that Paul simply welcomed this infirmity, whatever it was, with a clear sense of purpose. Initially, he begged for it to be taken away. His conclusion on the matter is some time after the initial onset of all this discomfort.

This accords with normal human experience. When something painful happens to us, we don't automatically accept it as sent from God. We think deeply about the issues. We accept what has happened, but we ask questions.

* What is God saying to me in this situation?
* Is there something I can learn?
* Am I at fault in some way?
* Does God want to take this painful situation away from me?
* Will he give me strength to face up to it and live through it?

By contrast, the super-apostles of Paul's day had just one answer every time. Everyone can and should be healed. It wasn't true then, and it isn't true today. Of course God heals, but not everyone, every time. That is what Paul is saying. God makes sense of suffering and of death. That is why Jesus Christ is such good news to a suffering and a dying world.

Paul's sense of purpose is the result of mature reflection. He can recognise that God has not feather-bedded him, but has allowed such discomforts for ultimate good and development of maturity.

* Is there something happening to you at the moment, where similar questioning would be of real value?

Sometimes God wants to remove our discomforts from us. But there are other times, discomforting as they may be, when to remove them would do us more harm than good. Reflect on the value of the lessons you have learnt in adversity. Ask yourself if you are in a learning situation at the moment, and just what you should be facing up to.

## Frustration illustrated

'Three times I pleaded with the Lord to take it away from me' (2 Corinthians 12:8).

Paul faces up to the problem. Paul pleaded with God; and he pleaded three times. He doesn't tell us exactly how he prayed, but from the word 'pleaded' we can sense his urgency, his seriousness, and his sense of deeply felt need. He must have faced a great deal of frustration at his unanswered prayer, given the severity of whatever it was he was suffering. So he is likely to have shared his need with others. He will probably have asked them to pray with him and for him; and on three separate occasions, he laid his needs before God.

Maybe you or someone you know is in the same situation. You have been praying consistently, and asking God to move in some specific way. You have been greatly encouraged to hear of other people's answers to prayer. But you are coming to a point of confusion. Why is God not answering my prayers? Why does he seem to have gone silent?

Sometimes of course, we can get in the way of God's response. There may be some matter of holiness of life, or our relationships, or our obedience, which the Lord wants us to sort out first. But here, in Paul, is a person who has done all that, a person who wants to walk closely with God in his life; and God seems to be silent.

That silence only aggravates the pain. Prayer can appear unanswered. Paul's prayer for healing seemed to go unanswered. At such times of silence, waiting can be deeply frustrating and perplexing. 'Three times I pleaded with the Lord to take it away from me.'

## Sufficient grace

'Three times I pleaded with the Lord to take it away from me. But he said to me, "My grace is sufficient for you, for my power is made perfect in weakness." Therefore I will boast all the more gladly about my weaknesses, so that Christ's power may rest on me. That is why, for Christ's sake, I delight in weaknesses, in insults, in hardships, in persecutions, in diffilties. For when I am weak, then I am strong' (2 Corinthians 12:8–10).

Paul asked the Lord to remove whatever it was which was such a sadness to him. For a while the Lord did seem silent But in the end God did answer his prayer. It wasn't the answer he expected or wanted. He was asking for the infirmity to be taken away. The answer he eventually received was, however, the answer he needed. 'My grace is sufficient for you, for my power is made perfect in weakness.'

David Watson was one of the greatest evangelists and Christian leaders of recent years in this country. He was known all over the world as a remarkable speaker and teacher and leader of missions. Sadly, he contracted cancer in 1983, and later died from the disease.

A few weeks before he died, David Watson took part in some lunchtime services in the West End of London. He had

had a remarkable remission, and though he had some pain, he was still a wonderful communicator, and actually looked strikingly well. Many people were claiming that he had been healed; but he was completely realistic about what was happening to him. He knew that the cancer was going to come back.

At the first of those lunchtime services, pleased yet surprised at the vast crowd who had turned out to hear him, he remarked to one of his colleagues with a look of great depth in his face, 'They've only come to see Lazarus.'

David Watson died just a few weeks after that. Of course, everybody longs for healing. By his remark, David obviously understood the enthusiasm people have to witness a living miracle – to see a latter day Lazarus raised from the dead. Everybody was expecting David Watson to be healed; but he himself was realistic. He had tremendous faith in God's purposes. And, of course, it was right to pray for his healing. God was really glorified in David Watson's death. Though he had much pain and suffering, David was genuinely radiant and peaceful in his last days of life.

In those last few weeks, right up to the last moments of his life, David Watson fearlessly applied the truth of those words. 'My grace is sufficient for you, for my power is made perfect in weakness.'

## The all wise Father

When we are up against it in our lives, from where are we going to get our strength? Paul says 'When I am weak, then I am strong.'

When God lets difficult times pass our way, when he appears to hold back from changing the situation in the way we long him to do, we can be assured that his purposes are good. When we are weak and accept that weakness as from God, then we will actually find his strength to face whatever it is we have to pass through.

None of us can be immune from suffering. Someone who lost her husband said, 'We shared many happy times, but also so many difficulties too. And if I had never faced some of those difficulties then, in a way, I don't think I would be able to cope now.' Such a truth will find agreement in the experience of many. It goes back to the goodness of God, and the fact that he is our Heavenly Father, and that he is infinitely wise.

As a human father, with our three little girls, I am already learning that I have to stand back and watch. There are times when I have to watch them learning painful lessons. There are times when it would not be right for me to interfere and risk destroying the learning process. I feel I suffer almost as much as them when they get hurt emotionally or physically. Anyone who is a parent will know exactly the same experience. It is all for a greater good.

We are children of an infinitely loving Heavenly Father. Sometimes he has to watch us learn painful lessons. There are times when it would not be right for him to interfere and risk destroying the learning process; and those are often the times when we think we are facing unanswered prayer.

When prayer goes apparently unanswered, when you have prayed and prayed about something deeply important to you, then you can be pretty sure you are in the midst of a learning process, permitted by God for your ultimate good. It is of course your wisdom against his. But God sees everything whole. He sees from the beginning to the end, and he really does know what is best for you, in this life and the next.

Do then be encouraged. When you are weak you can be strong. It may be that you need to give up a wrong sense of struggle. If you have been longing and asking for some time now, but unanswered prayer is all you have to show for your inner searching, then it could be that God is saying to you exactly what he said to the Apostle Paul all those years ago, and what he has said to countless sons and daughters of God all the way down the centuries. If that is the case, then this will be his answer to your prayer 'My grace is sufficient for you, for my power is made perfect in weakness.'

# 11

# DISCOVERING IDENTITY

Losses of all kinds, the ferocious pace of twentieth century living, and the deeply discouraging times of pain, illness and other setbacks, all contribute generously and remorselessly to the raw material upon which depressive reactions so voraciously feed. As we have seen, these elements of depression have their specific spiritual dimension in addition to the other human dynamics at work in our lives. There is, however, a further dynamic at work which involves the human and the spiritual elements of our make-up. Doubts and uncertainties in this area are an important part of what is sometimes referred to as existential depression. It is, however, an issue of universal relevance and significance, both to the sufferer and to the apparently healthy. It is to do with the question of identity.

This search for identity is fundamental in normal human development, especially in adolescence and the early twenties, when a child's existence is being asserted as an independent role from its parents. There are, in addition, other aspects of our lives where questions of identity require thoughtful attention. The careful formulation of a real and durable sense of identity is just as important for the Christian.

There is a significant relationship between elements of stress and depression. That such elements can precipitate depressive reactions suggests that whatever can be done to minimise such pressure will help in managing a depressive temperament. A Christian can learn to develop a whole new perspective on issues like status, self image and success, which will help to keep at bay the discomforting reactions of stress and depression. When we fail to discover our true identity in Christ we are open to all kinds of external influences, all demanding our attention. Such influences may be anything but healthy. The follower of Jesus Christ lives in two worlds, with a human and spiritual awareness, with a directive not to 'conform any longer to the pattern of this world, but be transformed by the renewing of your mind' (Romans 12:2). For mental and spiritual health, wholeness and well being, it is therefore essential to pose the question, 'What does it really mean to be human and Christian at one and the same time?'

## Who am I?

Many find themselves involved in a confused inner struggle, aiming to resolve the deeply important question 'Who am I?' The question is often perceived in emotional, rather than intellectual terms. Unfortunately, at the feelings level there is no easy response. Straightforward answers, capable of being put into a sentence or two, are more likely to touch the world of intellectual fact only, rather than satisfy the inner existential cravings of a longing of spirit.

## Searching for purpose

Of course, the question 'Who am I?' does involve objective truth. I am a human being and not an impersonal mechanism. My aspirations to know the truth about myself and the world and universe I live in spring from the fact that I am made in the image of God the Creator. All this is objective truth and important. Christians will want to state clearly certain facts which affect the question of our actual and perceived identity at a fundamental level. But as a concern which often gives rise to profound inner questioning and spiritual discomfort, the issue is felt deep down within us, often with a great deal of inner concern. Many describe such a concern as a kind of restless longing for peace and stability within, sensing a growing need for a more definite sense of purpose.

It is indeed a strange feeling, a rumbling uncertainty, which mingles with half-perceived doubts as to whether you belong within yourself and within this world. Such experiences, common at some time in life to many of us, are all tied into this basic question of identity. If you have ever felt like that, whatever your age, you may well have discovered that becoming and being a Christian does not automatically answer these deep inner needs of ours. Changes need to happen within us if we are to find our true identity, and fully appreciate what it means to be a son or a daughter of the living God.

## Knowing me, knowing God

To know ourselves more fully, we have to come to know God more fully, for it is from him we derive our true identity as we are made in his image. It is the work of Jesus Christ through the Spirit to restore that tarnished and distorted image within us – since it has been marred by the fall, and needs a total renovation.

The derivation of human identity is all tied into the issue of models. We have thought about models earlier in chapter 7, to do with learning from our parents, but let's be clear we understand the principles at work here.

Most of us have some kind of hero figure at some point in life. This is someone who fascinates us so much, we almost idolise them. Certainly if at any time you have had a hero, you will have wanted to model yourself on them, for that is the natural reaction.

The television soap operas on both sides of the Atlantic

have clearly recognised this appetite for models, and romantic novelists and thriller writers have all taken full advantage of our predisposition to admiration, even adoration of those we admire. Sometimes in our wilder moments we identify so closely with someone we look up to that we aspire to actually be that person, even for a day.

Just as everyone at some point in life is likely to have their heroes, so at a more mature level, we all have our models, those people we admire and from whom we have learnt. This desire to model ourselves on someone else, though of course it can be taken to extremes, is given to us by God. We are made to be learners. From the moment a child is born, it learns from those around it. We are not pre-programmed machines. We learn our humanness from other human beings, who are our models. As we have seen, in the early stages, this means learning from our parents, and then later from the wider circle of those around us.

At this later stage, if the world around us is powerful enough in its values and goals, its model of humanness, its answer to the question 'Who am I?', its world view and values will deeply affect our feeling and our thinking which go to make up our true identity.

## Status, self image and success

Our Western culture, and our lives included, has become preoccupied with three areas of particular concern. They are status, self image and success. These are three of the most important issues affecting our sense of identity which have become dominating preoccupations of the Western world at the end of the twentieth century.

If our understanding of being fully human is to be Christian, as a follower of Jesus Christ, then we are constrained to look at his particular distinctive approach to these concerns of status, self image and success. Jesus' own life is a clear demonstration of his concern on these issues. We must therefore ask if there is a spirituality which embraces these concerns of our modern world and our own lives, which makes sense of being human and being Christian at the same time, and helps us to find ourselves, to discover peace and stability, which brings in its wake a sense of purpose and belonging.

## Is there a model for identity in being human and being Christian?

The New Testament insists we must have a model for humanness. It is indicated by the Apostle Paul in his famous passage about the humanity of Christ in Philippians 2:5–11. 'Your attitude should be the same as that of Christ Jesus' (Philippians 2:5). We are meant to be learners, for it is written into our createdness. We learn from the example of others. But the real question is, from whom are you learning, because there are so many different views on offer?

The learning process is extremely subtle. We take in a great deal of information and ideas unconsciously. Most of us can recite an advertising slogan or two, though we have never consciously learned them by heart. Much of our store of information we simply absorb. It is the same with attitudes. We absorb so many of our attitudes unconsciously from the world around us. It is almost impossible not to be affected by the strong views of the 'go for it', human potential approach to life, because television, advertising, the media in general, are saturated with it.

The contemporary world celebrates status, self image, and success. But to anyone who reads the New Testament, it must be obvious that our society today is saying vastly different things on those issues from the attitudes of Christ himself. There is an immense identity gap between the contemporary world and the world view of Jesus. So we must ask, is Jesus out of step with life as it really is? To make any kind of response to this issue, we will need to rediscover what

Jesus teaches on these matters, particularly by the way Jesus lived his life. For the Apostle Paul holds up the life of Jesus as a supreme example, in a specific sense as a model for being human and being Christian.

## Attitude to status

'Your attitude should be the same as that of Christ Jesus; who being in very nature God, did not consider equality with God something to be grasped ...' (Philippians 2:5–6).

Do you worry about status? Many of us do. Status is about our position in life, in our work, at home, in church, in the community; for some nationally, even internationally. But status is not just our position, it is also about how we are perceived, and how we wish to be perceived.

On a family holiday on the northern French coast, as most children do at some time, our children asked about the movement of the waves and the rhythm of the tides. A simple explanation of the unseen pull of the moon seemed to suffice. This was the lesson: there are unseen forces at work. In the same way, in our own lives, there are certain factors which drive us forward. There are unseen psychological and emotional forces which drive our behaviour.

We have all grown up with habits of mind and behaviour which are always seeking for gratification. They want to be satisfied. It is a fact of upbringing. Someone who received very little love from their parents when young may well grow up to over-actively seek acceptance and love and affection or just plain attention from others. Someone whose work and achievements were consistently undervalued, even at times scorned in those early years, could well turn out to be a person particularly concerned for status and the esteem of others. We are not prisoners of our past. But the past does to a certain extent mould us, both negatively and positively.

It is important to admit we have these inner needs. That

provides no reason for shame. They are not wrong needs as such, but there is a right way of handling them.

## Incarnation and identity

How should we consider this question of position in life and how we wish to be perceived? Our attitude to status should be the same as Jesus himself, who, though he was in the form of God, did not count equality with God a thing to be grasped.

This is the response of the New Testament, and the Apostle Paul holds up the incarnation, the fact of God becoming man in the divine human person of Jesus of Nazareth, as a model for our own humanness. It is to do with this attitude to status. Jesus was prepared to take many steps down from his rightful status as the God of glory in order to involve himself fully in our world. Paul is saying Jesus did not cling to his rights. He did not count equality with God a thing to be grasped.

If followers of Jesus are to take his model of humanness seriously, and apply the lessons of the incarnation with any rigour, then some thoughtful self examination needs to take place.

* How often do you fall back on what you consider are your rights?
* How frequently do you use your 'position' to enable you to advance yourself, or get your own way?

Anyone in a leadership position has to be very careful they don't start getting bossy. There is the classic way of clinging to your rights at work. 'Sorry boss – it's not my job, it's someone else's responsibility.' Rights are not wrong in themselves, nor is the suggestion that anyone should be exploited;

but there are many rights we cling to sometimes a little more tenaciously than we should.

* How do I want other people to see me?
* What is my deep down attitude to my rights?

These questions of status come sharply into focus when we realise we are meant to be modelling ourselves upon Jesus, who gives us a remarkably different alternative view on modelling our lives in the eyes of others.

Though our society places an incredible, and unrealistic weight upon status, the real value of status is an illusion. Like sand, it slips through your fingers. The pursuit of status can trap us emotionally and spiritually. So often we seek to gratify those inner longings of ours which pressure us into seeking it. In the end, status brings no real freedom. It is a kind of covetousness. It only brings disappointment, for it has no power to transform us within.

## Three directions

Jesus' very different attitude to status gives us three specific directions. First: we must realise that if we want an inner freedom which will make us available for God's purposes, we must determine not to be guided by status. Status does function in this way for so many of us; but clearly and distinctively, Jesus did not cling to his rights. We are being told to emulate him, for that is the way of freedom.

The second direction is that if you find yourself at the bottom of the ladder, rejected, misunderstood – and many of us at different times and in different ways have and do experience this – that is where Jesus voluntarily placed himself, right at the bottom. We should think twice before we bemoan our lack of status. Jesus' example is meant to teach us we do not need status to be fully human nor to be fully effective as people and for God.

The third direction by contrast concerns those of high standing. If your role in life involves some measure of high status, how can you learn from Jesus' attitude? When we receive status from others how we handle it is crucial. When the spotlight shines on you, who gets the glory?

Sir Adrian Boult was one of the truly great English conductors of the previous generation. He was a fine musician, and a very fine person, of remarkable grace and modesty. The composer Vaughan Williams entrusted him with many of his first performances.

Long after Vaughan Williams' death, Boult conducted a concert performance of Vaughan Williams' opera 'The Pilgrims Progress' at London's Festival Hall. It was quite an event. It was the first public performance since the première some twenty years before. There was a terrific ovation. The gracious old man – he was in his eighties – lifted up the massive full score way above his head, while the applause was echoing enthusiastically round the concert hall. It was quite clear what he meant, and quite clear who should get the glory.

So the question for anyone involved in a position of high status is who gets the glory when the spotlight shines? Those in the arts, those in the public eye, sportsmen, leaders and high achievers of all sorts have to watch their craving for glory. Such a craving has a right and a wrong way of being handled. Jesus' way is to deflect the glory, and it is a practical way which we can emulate.


## Approach to self image


He 'made himself nothing, taking the very nature of a servant, being made in human likeness' (Philippians 2:7).

When Paul talks about Jesus making himself nothing, it is rich and striking language. The Greek word *kenosis* means 'to empty'. What did Jesus empty himself of? He emptied himself of his glory, and by contrast took on the form of a servant. It is not unrealistic to say that Jesus changed his self image, the way he saw himself and the way he wished to be seen.

Self image is the way we see ourselves. For some of us our self image is a bit jangled. We don't like ourselves over much. That is why we are over concerned for status, or for others to see us in a particular way. We tend to hide what we rightly or wrongly think is the truth about ourselves from others. As valuable as all the psychological paraphernalia about self image may be, nonetheless the concern here is different. It is not so much that we should account for our wrong or distorted view of ourselves, but that we should take on a right and pure view or goal for its expression in our lives. Jesus' own self image has a practical consequence. How we see ourselves should determine what we are in practice. And the word servant here is the central issue.

## The servant role

The most detailed prophetic description of Jesus in the Old Testament is of the suffering servant in Isaiah 53. Jesus said of himself, 'the Son of Man did not come to be served, but to serve, and to give his life as a ransom for many' (Matthew 20:28).

* How would you summarise your role attitude to life?
* Do you see yourself as a servant, of God and of others?

This servant mentality is essential for our self image, if we are going to be real followers of Jesus Christ in practice. The world does not applaud the concept of servanthood. Instinctively, we don't like it, because we are fallen beings, and our lives are out of step with God's purposes. But God's way reverses human values. It is the way Jesus chose, and it is the way of freedom. If you are a Christian, whether you have been a Christian just a few days or many years, what is God saying to you about areas in your life where in practice you can be like Jesus, a servant? The world says, 'be served'. God says, 'you serve, and be like Christ'.

Jesus' approach to self image was to see himself in the way he wished to express himself in practice in his life. His self image, as ours should be as his followers, is that of a servant.

## Understanding success

'And being found in appearance as a man, he humbled himself and became obedient to death – even death on a cross!' (Philippians 2:8).

Modelling ourselves on Jesus means learning from him, admiring the richness of his humanness, and seeing in him a pattern for our own. So when Paul says, 'your attitude should be the same as that of Christ', it must involve Jesus' understanding of success.

Success and the world of advertising belong together. It is not surprising that advertising has become one of the fastest growth industries in both Europe and the USA in the past few years. The general idea of all advertising is to create as high a profile for a product or individual as possible; to move them to the front of the queue; to create a demand; to boost the image.

This is one way of success, the commercial way. But if you are to be used by God, there is a different approach altogether. It reverses the normal values to which we have become used. You wouldn't think that humbling yourself and becoming obedient could produce success. But where God is concerned, it is humility and obedience which belong together. The one depends on the other.

The words of John the Baptist remind us of this truth, as he referred to Jesus 'I must decrease, he must increase.' You do have to humble yourself, in order to be obedient. But so many of us get the wrong picture in our mind at this point. Humbling yourself is not that odious, pathetic, self deprecating attitude, which is sadly seen amongst Christians of a certain outlook, a ghastly caricature of what true humanity is all about. Humbling yourself means that you let your self concern decrease, that your concern for God may increase.

We are all dominated to a greater or lesser extent by our selves. We are preoccupied by our concern to do well, to advance our own cause, to be a success. But Jesus' way is different. He shows us we have to make room for God's concerns, and then we have to learn to be obedient. It is no use pretending this is a popular way of looking at life. You wouldn't believe it to be the way of success for it runs counter to the popular approach we are so used to seeing in the world around us. Yet Jesus humbled himself and became obedient, in his case right to the point of death.

So who said this thorough re-working of our inner attitudes was going to be easy? It certainly was not for Jesus. He gave the utmost. But if we ask what it really means to be human and Christian at the same time, we must accept that the most effective way to discover our most enriched humanness will also involve the shedding of cherished wrong approaches. It involves taking Jesus' example not just seriously and with admiration, but taking on his attitudes as our own overall life pattern which must mean some considerable personal adjustments.

## True spirituality

'Therefore God exalted him to the highest place, and gave him the name that is above every name, that at the name of Jesus every knee should bow, in heaven and on earth and under the earth, and every tongue confess that Jesus Christ is Lord, to the glory of God the Father' (Philippians 2:9–11).

From where should we derive a pattern, a model for our humanness? Paul's answer is to have the same attitude, the same mind as Jesus Christ. But what about status, self image, success? Jesus clearly reverses what people stand for today. Yet the overwhelming conclusion of Paul's teaching is that it is for this very reason that 'God exalted him to the highest place.' And it is this question of spirituality which we must investigate further.

That difference between Jesus' attitude and the values of a secular humanist culture is plain to see. We aim first of all to satisfy our needs. It was not that Jesus did not have inner needs. He was human, he had the same human longings as any of us. The vital difference is, he set his own need on one side. He gave himself wholeheartedly to God's purposes. Such an approach will always feel like a risk. This kind of faith to put such an approach into action always demands a great deal of courage. Yet Paul states with a genuine sense of triumph the actual consequences of this radical approach to values which we are being asked to follow.

'God exalted him to the highest place.' That must be the foundation of our spirituality, to believe that it is God who exalts. God raises people up. In the final and most lasting sense, it is God who gives success.

If we are being encouraged to model and pattern our lives on Jesus – to be human and to be Christian, it does mean taking on an upside down set of values. It will mean being radically different from the way our fellow human beings conduct their lives. It means taking the hard way out, when the going could be easy. It means taking the flak and the criticisms from others; from your family, the people you work with, even your friends. It means facing up to the pressures which will come to you powerfully from within, as your own inner cravings cry out for fulfilment. We cannot escape it. It means being a servant. It means becoming obedient to God. It is a very different way of living.

In these words, 'Your attitude should be the same as that of Christ Jesus', we are being asked to take on a model for humanness. This will profoundly challenge us on our attitudes to status, self image, success, spirituality. It provides us with a strengthening of our inner attitudes to bring us more into line with God's purposes for our lives, avoiding that which can be so damaging to our sense of ease within.

None of us can grow to become truly human, unless we wholeheartedly take on this upside down way of seeing things which is Jesus' pattern for living. Humility, obedience, servanthood is the life style above all which God exalts. It enables us not only to answer who we are, and to transcend the pressures around us, but to become who we are meant to be. To be human and to be Christian.

Part Five

# The Healing Process

# 12

# WHEN HELP IS NEEDED

Depression is a difficult human state about which to generalise. Someone's mild attack of the blues may make them feel wretched enough for a day or so, but they are perhaps soon restored to cheerful, purposeful activity. Yet another person can feel gloomy and increasingly ineffective in personal terms, and with the progress of the weeks they may well find themselves unable to effect any useful and lasting change in their perplexing condition.

Because the overcoming of depression does not fit neatly into one single mode of treatment, there are times when outside help is clearly indicated for depressive conditions. It is important to crack the myth that we should always be able to control the way we feel. It is simply not true where certain kinds of depression are concerned. The frustration and guilt can build up alarmingly when this untruth is allowed continuing and misinformed existence.

Christians who become depressed sometimes receive the impression from the well meaning that if they would only have more faith in the loving purposes of God, all would be well. As we have already seen, such dynamics of love and purpose are indeed remarkably powerful in their truth and spiritual impact. But what about those times when all the wisdom available to us seems to make such little difference?

## Seeking help

It should by now be obvious that there are clearly times when skilled outside help is needed. Family doctors, Christian

ministers, and other counsellors are all well used to giving
help in such circumstances; in addition, when there is serious
concern for someone's safety and well being, GPs, the Police,
the Samaritans, Clergy and others will all advise and help in
potential suicide situations. But what about other kinds of
help? What use are drugs and other physical treatments.
What about the famous analyst's couch? Can I actually be
talked out of what is distressing me?

## Taking treatment

For many who are depressed, the family doctor will be the
first port of call. It is really worth cultivating a good relationship with your doctor. The vast majority of GPs are
skilled and caring, and though they are much in demand, you
can always ask for a longer appointment if you need more
time to explain your situation and needs. You can also ask for
a referral to a psychiatrist if you want another opinion. If
you happen to be one of the few unfortunate ones who
simply cannot get on with your GP for some reason, then
it is perfectly within your rights to seek to change your
doctor.

Your doctor will prescribe medical treatment if he thinks it
is absolutely necessary. Trust his or her clinical judgement.
It is, as always, a matter of matching the medicine to the
illness. Endogenous depression requires the use of anti-
depressants for no other treatment is likely to make much
impact. This is because the root of the problem lies in
disordered brain chemistry. Some severe reactive de-
pressions also benefit from such treatment, because of the
corresponding chemical changes caused by long term
depressive conditions.

Deep issues of personal conflict cannot, however, be removed by taking tablets. There is an interesting feature,
however, where severe conflict is present in chemically orig-
inated endogenous depression. Given such a condition, no

amount of careful and skilled talking will successfully release the pressure and difficulties of these conflicts. Indeed, the sufferer may have managed perfectly well with these issues before becoming ill. Why is he now unable to cope or overcome?

The answer is to do with his disordered biochemistry. Here drugs such as tricyclic or tetracyclic anti-depressants, (which work by increasing the quantity of monoamine neurotransmitters in the brain, thus helping the brain to replenish its diminished store of monoamines due to depression) or perhaps a monoamine oxidase inhibitor (which inhibits the enzyme which destroys monoamines, with similar effect) are the treatment of choice. In some cases, they begin to give relief as soon as a fortnight after commencing a course of treatment.

Because these drugs can have some discomforting side effects, some people make the mistake of dropping the treatment before it has had a chance to give its benefit. If you are prescribed drugs like these, it is vital to give them the time your doctor indicates. Where there are any doubts as to the best method of treatment, ask your doctor if he can refer you to seek the advice of an experienced psychiatrist.

Some recurrent depression, and certainly manic depressive psychosis, can also benefit from preventative treatment by taking lithium carbonate. No one really knows why this simple salt is so effective in controlling and preventing recurrent depression and mania. It has however to be carefully monitored in its use, with regular blood tests.

Electro-convulsive therapy (ECT) has been a life saver for some extremely severe sufferers. A hundred volt electric shock is administered to the brain, producing a temporary epilepsy. It is a severe form of treatment, with a very bad public image, mainly because of its misuse and abuse in certain parts of the world. Its use today bears very little resemblance to what was seen on the cinema screens some years ago in the controversial film *One Flew over the Cuckoo's Nest*. Again, the effectiveness of ECT is recognised without its workings being fully understood. It has great value in the most severe cases of depression where a psychiatrist's special knowledge, experience, and fine judgement indicate the appropriateness of this treatment.

## The talking cures

Finding someone suitably skilled to talk to is certainly the first approach to healing for most people. Whereas psychiatrists deal in drugs and other physical treatments, they are not so naive as to suppose that for most people the best cure comes in a capsule. Like many other helping professionals they spend a great deal of time talking people through the problems of their lives.

## The counselling market place

A difficulty these days is the embarrassment of riches. To whom should you turn if you need help with some of the problems we are discussing? If you are facing depression and are needing help, there is never any harm in getting your doctor to check you out physically. Some clue may emerge at that stage. If, however, you are thrown back on your own devices, to whom should you turn?

There are so many therapies and therapists around these days that it is as well to avoid the cranks. Avoid, too, the easy promises of the cults, and other groups which offer quick and apparently swiftly effective solutions.

It is important to have someone who will really listen to you and draw you out. Beware the counsellor that does all the talking. He shouldn't be saying very much at all if you are really going to gain insight into your self. Don't expect much straight advice, either. A skilled counsellor will help you to come to your own decisions, simply helping you to see clearly the implications of all the alternatives before you.

Many major cities and towns have professional counsellors who are Christians working in a counselling agency. London's Care and Counsel is just one example. Local churches can usually recommend an effective professional working locally. Sometimes a caring, thoughtful friend can be of immense support. It is certainly the case that the personality and life experience of the counsellor matters as much as his or her formal training.

One of the main helps that skilled counsellors, therapists, or analysts can give is in the area of abreaction. Abreaction means the reliving of a painful emotional experience, sometimes otherwise forgotten, to release the emotion which never before found full and adequate expression. Sometimes we are reluctant to 'go over the past'. The thought is often painful. Yet there can be immense relief when this happens in a caring and properly controlled way. However it does again emphasise the need for a trusting relationship between the counsellee and counsellor. Do not despise the value of talking over a cup of tea with someone you dearly trust, and who is able to help you by their sensitive listening. It is just as much therapy, as anything more professional or expensive.

Many Western societies are becoming increasingly isolated, so that the kind of care at one time informally available in caring communities, is now solely in the hands of the professionally qualified. We do need to recover not only the skills of listening, but also the means to extend effective care, especially to those who are in emotional need and require such support from sensitive and caring listeners.

## Who cares about caring?

Christians have a distinct practical responsibility in this area of caring for people in need. Jesus is clear that in several distinctive ways his followers should take the lead when it comes to caring. His own teaching suggests that the Christian Church should be in the forefront when it comes to

caring for individuals. 'A new commandment I give you:
Love one another. As I have loved you, so you must love one
another. By this all men will know that you are my disciples,
if you love one another' (John 13:34–35).

## The importance of care

Jesus' concern is not merely a hope, an aspiration or a
preference. Jesus is insistent about care, for the form of his
words is as a commandment.

What does this command teach us about care, and why is
it 'new'? This is the only new commandment, on a level with
the ten commandments given through Moses, which Jesus
ever gave. In a sense, it is commandment number 11. Jesus
clearly regards it as of the utmost importance, for the new
command involves a new responsibility to love one another.
Jesus is emphasising we should be more concerned with
giving than receiving when it comes to the exercise of love
and care.

In Jesus' time there is evidence to suggest that pastoral
care was exercised through the levitical priesthood; this was
a development in the period between the Old and New
Testaments. The emphasis was on receiving. Only the
priests did the caring. The average person was passive, and
received the care, but did little if anything to give care to
others. Jesus turns that upside down. He says we have to take
responsibility for each other, for all of us have to learn to
give in terms of care. According to Jesus, the true goal for
his followers is to love and care for one another; not to
expect someone else to do it, but to get on with doing it for
ourselves.

There are still people today who want to wriggle out of that
responsibility. Of course, it is so much easier to say: here's a
doctor, a social worker, a clergyman, let them do the caring.
We've other things to do, let the professionals do it, they
are paid after all. But Jesus is saying the opposite; in

consequence we need to work at applying his words to the increasingly depersonalised and professionalised world in which we live today. All of us have the ability to listen. The art of listening sensitively, communicating acceptance, warmth and concern is of immense help to someone facing depression. It is an art which anyone can exercise, and is in itself an expression of love.

Jesus uses the word 'love' to characterise Christian care. Love is a practical word referring to how we treat each other. We all have a responsibility to care for each other, with the depth of commitment the word 'love' implies.

Human beings need love as much as food. The human spirit shrivels and dies without it. The absence of love causes all sorts of self doubts and inner torments. Yet love costs nothing, and with it so much help can be given to others in need.

## A model for care

Models give us a standard by which to measure our own behaviour and performance. Christians should always be seeking to model themselves on Jesus. In the Gospels one of the most common pictures of Jesus is to see him caring for others. It is clear from his words that Jesus wants the love of his followers for each other to be so close to his love for us that people will hardly be able to tell the difference. In this way Jesus puts himself forward as a model for love. 'As I have loved you, so you must love one another.'

* Do you have a receiving or a giving attitude to care?
* Do you expect others to serve you?
* Do you do all you can to serve others?
* Are you prepared to work at becoming a patient listener?
* How are you learning from Jesus' model of love and care?

All this comes as an immense challenge to Christians to discover and sharpen their gifts of care. So many problems which people face daily in their lives, which sometimes grow to pathological proportions, could have well been stemmed early on had there been caring intervention from family, friends and neighbours. Of course we need the professionals too; but they are often brought in at a late stage when much suffering could have been avoided.

The New Testament is clear that there are two levels of care that Christians should be able to offer. They are general care and special care. General care is what we can all do. We can all take grapes when someone's not well; we can pray with our friends; we can help with the shopping or sort out a practical problem; we can drink tea and listen; we can befriend when there's loneliness; we can be compassionate when there's sadness.

Special care implies specific gifts for care. This is one aspect of the gifts of healing mentioned by Paul in 1 Corinthians 12:9. So there will always be some Christians gifted by God for special care purposes. These are people who are good at coping with crises; people who can help with strained relationships; people with special gifts of wisdom; people with listening and counselling skills; people who can effectively support the long term sick; people above all who will bring the word of Christ and the comfort of the Spirit to each person and situation as they have need.

## Helping you

When help is needed it is a matter of matching the help to the need. Don't be afraid of seeking help. Put your pride or your fears on one side. Many have trod this path before you, and much can be done to help you. Good and able people become depressed. Much of what you are feeling negatively about yourself may relate to real experiences, but is equally likely to be emotionally distorted by your depressed condition. It is not as hopeless as you no doubt feel it is. Take the helping hand, and let God's healing for you be mediated through whatever in his grace he is providing for your need.

# 13

# SELF HELP AND HELPING OTHERS

Taking full responsibility for our selves is an important dimension in the management of our mental, physical and spiritual needs. There is much we can all do to ensure that our sense of health and well being is fully supported and maintained. Helping others too is just as much a responsibility. If we should be called upon to help a friend or relative who finds themselves in need, then we will need to be prepared. This means discovering what is of most use in either preventing or reducing the impact of depressive episodes. The knowledge needed for effective self help and the helping of others overlaps in many complementary ways. If you know how to look after your own house, you'll turn out to be the wise neighbour who can be trusted in times of need.

## Both ends of the candle

Keith is a very bright 22-year-old student. He has been subject to bouts of depressive moodiness since he was in his mid-teens. His doctor feels it is much to do with his personality and upbringing. Keith had an unsettled childhood, three times facing the trauma of moving from one foster home to another. He drives himself in order to prove his worth. It is of first importance to him to receive esteem from others; his academic achievements are a particular means he only half consciously uses to achieve this.

Keith should not be having too much difficulty for his

finals, as his college has a continuous assessment system, and he is already well ahead with his work and standard. Yet Keith has been consistently burning the candle at both ends. He is up at the crack of dawn, and stays up into the early hours. Practically all his time is spent in the college library preparing his final year thesis. He doesn't break for lunch. Some chocolate and regular supplies of coffee see him through till supper time, when he usually grabs a stale sandwich from the bar with more beer than does his waistline good.

Friends who suggest that Keith should have a more balanced lifestyle and diet, are greeted with amused disdain. Keith is driven by his need to succeed in his academic accomplishments. He thinks little about health issues. His only concern is to keep up the pace, and try and rid himself of the slowness, anxiety and moodiness which is like a dog at his heels.

The term is not by any means over, when Keith's friends notice the tired eyes, the slow manner, and the wearied approach to his work, as Keith begins to suffer the same old bouts of the blues which have been his unwelcome and recurring life story for so many years.

## Help yourself

If, like Keith, we are prone to depressive episodes, is there anything we can do to help ourselves? Because of the slowing effect of depression, whatever its form or origin, many people give up any hope of being able either to prevent its appearance, or to improve the situation once it begins to make itself felt. There is, however, much that we can do to help ourselves, involving both self knowledge and the practical application of straightforward life principles.

Keith's predisposition to depression will clearly be helped by coming more to terms with his image of himself. His need for esteem is understandable, given his unsettled childhood and background. This is the root cause, but what can he do in the meantime? Some analysis of Keith's lifestyle will give us some helpful directions for exploring our own.

### Attitudes

Keith is a perfectionist, with a low self image who craves love and esteem from others. Like many highly motivated people, his attitudes are mildly obsessional.

### Lifestyle

Keith rises early and retires late. His daily existence is monochrome, dominated by his library study and his exclusive concern for exam success.

### Health

Keith's diet is nutritionally unbalanced, with a concentration on sugars, fats, caffeine and alcohol, to the exclusion of adequate protein, vitamins and fibre from fresh food. He also eats irregularly. Keith's exercise is minimal.

## Counting the cost

Given such an approach to daily life, it is not surprising that the onset of a depressive episode is made much worse. It is arguable whether failures in effective self management actually contribute to the initial onset of the depression, but in many cases, depending on the nature of the depression, this will certainly play its part. There is an undoubted link between recovery from depression and effective life and health care.

## Life rhythms

Keith made matters far worse for himself than he needed to. He is an intelligent student. He knows he has a tendency to perfectionism, and that he is obsessional over academic achievement. He knows that he tends to drive himself. He could take a firm hold and ask himself if it is really necessary to work with such pent up energy and concern, especially as this puts his health at risk when he does. He could look at his lifestyle and realise the lack of sense in robbing himself of rest and exercise. The body needs rhythms of activity, rest and sleep for proper health. The same approach would apply to his diet which is essential if his mental life is to be in proper equilibrium. As for his monochrome lifestyle, it is a case of 'All work and no play makes Jack a dull boy.' The mind needs properly paced rhythms as much as the body. One continual focus is a recipe for a stale spirit.

## Looking after Number 1

What are the most important elements to look out for in effective self care? We have to remember to care for the whole person, and not look at ourselves through too narrow a focus. Effective self care will therefore involve health, sociability, emotions and attitudes, personal planning, spirituality, and self encouragement.

## Healthcare – diet and exercise

We have already seen how Keith abused his diet and exercise needs. Not many people in the West are protein deficient, but we all eat far too many junk foods, refined food products, white sugar, salt, and chemical additives and saturated fats. Our emphasis on refined products, especially white bread and white rice, and our relative neglect of fresh vegetables, beans and pulses means that the average daily consumption of fibre in the British diet is only 20g. As this is an average figure, with some this means as little as 6g a day. This contrasts vividly with figures of between 40g to 60g for daily consumption in the Third World, where there is, in consequence, considerably less incidence of many of the disabling and life threatening diseases which afflict us in the West. These diseases of affluence include coronary heart disease, cancer of the large bowel, diverticular disease, as well as several other related conditions, and the all too prevalent Western problem of constipation with all its attendant health risks. Obesity is a major Western problem too, with 40% of adults in Europe and North America, being overweight.

Nobody claims that eating bran for breakfast is going to cure depression! However, a more healthy approach to diet will help a great deal to put the body into good shape so that it is able to function as healthily as possible. This will help avoid the debilitating effects of poor or irregular nourishment which is such a common element today. All of us need to learn to eat for health, and not simply for pleasure. We need to reduce saturated fats drastically. White bread, white flour, white rice and white pasta, and white sugar are nutritional trouble spots, badly deficient in fibre and essential nutrients.

Try switching to wholemeal bread, brown rice and pasta, fresh fruit and vegetables, skimmed milk and margarine rich in polyunsaturates. Watch your intake of red meats, and add fish and beans to your repertoire as well. Try and reduce your caffeine intake, and if you drink alcohol, don't forget it is high in calories, and the British government's recommended maximum weekly figures are 16 units for a man or 8 units for a woman, where a unit is equivalent to a small glass of wine, or half a pint of beer.

Many people who get depressed eat for comfort. For some

this may mean unwelcome weight gain. You may need to lose weight. If you do, the best way is not to fall for the meal replacement, magic pills and potions way. Talk to your doctor first, decide on your goal weight, and then gradually aim to take off the pounds by a fully nutritious diet, but being sparing with the fats and sugars. An average weight loss of between one to two pounds a week is plenty, otherwise you'll be losing muscle tissue as well as fat!

There is no better way to diet than to plan your meals thoroughly and with care for their nutritional balance, with ample amounts of fibre to fill you up and protect your health. Get a comprehensive calorie chart. Weigh everything and count everything, write it down, and be strong. You will soon be amply rewarded for your strength of character. You can do it. If you do need to diet, then the improvement in your self image, not to mention your mirror image, will be considerable.

All this will be helped by exercise. Exercise generally is good for the mind and spirit as well as the body. Though it takes about 35 miles of brisk walking to lose a pound of fat, half an hour to forty five minutes of fast daily walking will keep off a weight gain of up to three and half stone. This is particularly significant when weight loss has been achieved, for as many sadly know, it is only too easy to quickly gain what so much effort took to lose. The factor at work behind all this is our body's metabolic rate.

When you diet, your body adjusts automatically to the decreased intake of calories. The metabolic rate slows, so over a period of time you need less and less food intake to meet your energy requirements, and it is therefore increasingly difficult to get rid of unwanted pounds. However, exercise speeds up the rate of body calorie consumption. So regular exercise is a must for weight loss, and its maintenance, as well as for maintaining an efficient healthy system. Any exercise which propels your body through air or water is of real benefit. Find something to suit you. Don't despise regular walking though. It is one of the best ways to exercise simply, easily, and effectively.

* Do you need to take any action on your diet or exercise pattern?

## Sociability – friends and relaxation

How sociable are you? It is true that when depression strikes, your desire to mix with friends can hit rock bottom. These are the times when social confidence ebbs away, and nervousness, diffidence and shyness in company is the distressing norm of social relationships.

We all need each other for a variety of reasons. Part of this is to do with our basic needs to give and receive love at a variety of levels. Friends are those people who know and accept the real you. You can be yourself with your friends, and you can contribute just as much to their happiness and fulfilment.

For friendship to go deep it is not just a meeting of minds, it is as much the sharing of experiences which lends the bonding effect. When you share experiences, you build up a fund of common memories which gives richness and personal quality to the relationships. This in itself creates belonging which is a basic human need.

We neglect to work at friendships at our peril. Ruth, a departmental head of a national building society, is in her early fifties and unmarried. Her mother died just recently after a long and protracted illness. It was regarded by Ruth as a release for her mother, and she is getting herself back to normal now. Ruth is not a very sociable person outside of the office. In her busy and stimulating work she has felt for many years that she has ample contact with her staff with whom she gets on very well.

Ruth has lost the art of cultivating friendships as such, since there is ample to do and to talk about at work. Though she is quite accepting of her singleness, there has come a point in Ruth's life where she has been experiencing a distinct loneliness of spirit. There is always someone to talk

to, yet Ruth's relationships seem to function only on a work
level. People in her office always say that Ruth keeps her
distance. The truth is Ruth would like to get closer, but has
neglected her opportunities. Until her mother died, Ruth
hadn't realised how important friendships are.

* Do you cultivate your friendships?
* Do you give time for shared activities?

## Emotions – check those attitudes

We dealt with understanding the past and resolving painful
memories in chapters three and four. You'll find it helpful to
go back to those chapters to review some of the insights and
the exercises there.

Just as on a diet, after the weight loss is complete, you
have to continue consciously to work hard to properly maintain the new slimmer, fitter you; in a similar way, we have to
do the same with our attitudes, once we have done some work
on them.

Janet had a particular problem with guilt feelings. When
she became mildly depressed from time to time, the guilt
feelings would bang away in her like the clanging of old tin
cans. Janet was much helped when she became a Christian
to know that she was a new person in Christ. Forgiveness
meant a great deal to her. However, old habits die hard.
The new-born Christian soon found that the old voice of
accusation still bothered her.

It was worst in the morning when sometimes Janet felt that
she could hardly face the day. Talking to her minister about
this, a way of handling the feelings became apparent. Her
minister advised her to say to herself on waking, before any
other thoughts occurred to her, 'I am forgiven, I am
accepted, and God loves me totally.' She was to remind
herself of this great fact of her salvation several times over,

and then praise and thank God because it is true. He then told her actively to refuse to listen to the guilt feelings since they did not any longer correspond to what is true. In this way Janet gradually broke her habit of mind; but it was necessary to do an occasional minor overhaul when the old attitudes paid a fleeting visit.

We all have to watch our attitudes whatever they may be. Our emotions have a habit of returning to well trodden paths. Since, as has already been pointed out, our emotions are an unreliable guide to the way things may actually be, it is as well to keep on checking up on ourselves. A good rule of thumb is to ask: 'What has been my dominant attitude over the last month?' It may have been positive or negative, cheerful or miserable, appreciative or critical, celebratory or threatened. Keep a watch on your emotional attitudes, and you will be that much more settled within.

## Personal planning – organising yourself

In the next chapter there will be material to help in the specific planning of personal goals. But there are many ways in which we need to consider the planning of our lives for health and well being.

How seriously do you plan ahead to make the most of your time off? If you are a person with time on your hands, how actively do you aim to use your diary to space out interesting and fulfilling activities? It is so much easier to organise outings with friends or family if you book up in advance. You'll have something to which to look forward, and something definite planned.

Holidays are a most valued break in the daily routine. If you are able, it is well worth saving up, and doing something worthwhile. It is a good investment in your health. Short weekend breaks, and days away all contribute to the wider perspectives brought by stimulating times of relaxation.

## Spirituality – prayer and worship

It is not possible to be fully human unless we recognise God's claim upon our lives. He is our maker and Jesus Christ is our saviour. We come into a living relationship with God as our Father, when we put our active trust in Jesus for forgiveness of our sins, and the strength and power of the Holy Spirit.

If you are a committed Christian, do you have a regular daily time of prayer and Bible study? It will help you so much to do so. You'll need some Bible study notes to help you, such as those provided by the Scripture Union. It is best not to be over ambitious to start off with. Start with a period of quiet of about seven minutes, and work up from there. If you keep a note book too, then you can jot down what you have learnt from the Bible, as well as recording requests for prayer, and the answers as they follow.

Everyone has to find their own manner of having what some Christians call a 'quiet time'. Time spent with God develops your relationship with him and builds you up in spirit just as much as other activities have a beneficial effect on your body. So it is also important to meet regularly with other Christians, on Sundays, for worship and ministry, and during the week, for fellowship, prayer and Bible study. In addition, finding your own way of using your gifts for Christian service, within the church, as well as giving to the Lord's work are important elements in living out all the God-planned means of ensuring spiritual health and vigour.

## Self encouragement

In all these ways, do remember to be kind to yourself. You don't have to indulge your whims, but neither do you need to be hard and ungenerous to yourself. Do you know what really brings you pleasure and a sense of ease? If it is cuddling up in bed with a favourite romantic novel or a thriller, give yourself a break, you could probably do with the diversion. If it is listening to loud music over the headphones, or an hour spent quietly gardening, do it if you know it does you good. If it is going for a long walk in the country, or an afternoon spent in a DIY store, then it will be of benefit to take the opportunity afforded by the break in your routine.

God made this world to be enjoyed. To take pleasure in creation is something which fulfils our humanness. Those facing depression will be slipping into the grey, colourless area of experience. To keep your self stimulated will help you to avoid this shift, and to climb out of the milder form of depressive experience.

## Helping a friend

Everything that has been said so far will also assist in giving help and support to a friend in need. The biggest requirement in the helping of others is to be a good listener, and the greatest personal quality is that of warm understanding acceptance.

Listening is an under rated and under practised art. Most of us are not good at listening without interrupting. In daily conversation we will often fail to let someone finish what they are wanting to say. Our minds race ahead with thoughts, questions or ideas of our own. When someone tells us about themselves, we may quickly be wanting to turn the conversation round to us. Sometimes the reason is we think we know what they are going to say, long before they get to the point. Other times it is simply impatience, boredom, or plain bad manners!

All these habits of discourse are a positive impediment when it comes to the creative listening needed in helping with depression. A 'sympathetic hearing' is not so much that the one who listens to you agrees with everything you say; it is far more to do with the sense of having been thoroughly listened to and genuinely understood. It is important that what you have said has been accepted and respected, with a sense of identification with any emotions which have been expressed, be they joy, pain, happiness or sadness. To be listened to in this deeper sense is of very great value, as it not only values and recognises your full personhood, it also fulfils a basic human need to communicate not just fact but emotion.

If the listener is not thoroughly attuned and centred on the person who is speaking, communication is frustrated and ineffective, and rebounds on the communicator. All of us know when we have been listened to; it is an uplifting experience. The opposite, unfortunately is also true. This is all the more serious in depression, since the depressed often have trouble putting what they want to say into words; they may be repetitive, monosyllabic, and only succeed at giving a hint at what they truly want to say. How much more frustrating when you are in true need, to find yourself 'rejected' by a careless listener.

## Effective listening

Listening to what people say and listening to what they are feeling is a different matter. Most of us realise that human discourse is far more complex than the simple communication of factual data. Fifty per cent of our communication is non verbal, finding expression on our faces and the movements, shapes and poses of our bodies. Yet much of our body and verbal language is given over to the expression or the hinted expression of emotion. How, then, can we become more effective listeners? There are no secrets as such, but practice makes such a difference.

### Concentration

Concentration requires practice, so try this very simple exercise to boost your concentration skills. Shut your eyes and concentrate on any sound outside of yourself for about half a minute. Did your concentration wander? Now switch your concentration to your heartbeat, for about the same time, and then to your breathing. When your time is up, concentrate again on something outside yourself.

You will find you can only concentrate on one thing at a time with full attention. It is the same with human converse. So use this concentration exercise regularly to firm up your resistance to distraction, either from outside stimuli, or your own inner thoughts. It will help to do it in a bus queue, or in the street, or anywhere where there are natural distractions, as such techniques need to be sharpened in the real world where they will need to be exercised.

*Tuning in*

When you next have a thoughtful conversation with anyone, aim to tune in to their wavelength. This means giving them your total concentration, not interrupting, leaving silences as breathing points, if it seems possible they may add something of significance, before you respond. Avoid expressing your own opinion, instead aim to reflect back to them what they have said, thus showing that you understand what they are saying, and encouraging them to continue.

## Paraphrasing

Putting what you have heard back into different words can be helpful, but it can also appear trite. Its value lies in showing the person in need that you are actively listening, and have understood what they are saying. Part of its function is to clarify statements which have been made, sometimes encouraging the speaker to describe more deeply or fully what is being spoken of. Paraphrasing is especially valuable when some emotional response has been expressed. If someone says, 'I feel all keyed up about going to the meeting tonight. It's making me feel sick,' the response can be a question. 'Does it make you feel stressed and tight inside?' The paraphrase response shows empathic understanding. Similarly if someone speaks of something very painful in their lives, the response of understanding should show on the face, maybe with some other appropriate body gesture, as well as in words.

'Feeling like this, I've even wondered about ending my life.'

'It must be a very black experience for you. You must have some really wretched moments . . .'

It is good to work on finding matching expressions for common emotions. These can build your vocabulary for effective paraphrasing. Find either synonyms or metaphors for expressions of happiness, sadness, fear, pain, panic, despair, frustration, anger. Try and make as comprehensive a list as you can, and think of other relevant emotions and work on these too.

## Avoiding prejudice

We all have our own thoughts and points of view. We also have our own prejudices. All kinds of people came to Jesus for help. None was turned away. Jesus had a clear understanding of God's will and ways, but he was not prejudiced against any individuals. Most of us do have prejudices, and they will potentially spoil the effectiveness of the help we can give to others.

Make a list of the kinds of things you most dislike about people, and those who annoy you most. Once you are aware of such feelings within yourself, you will be helped in not letting them become too much of a distraction for you as a listener. Ask God to liberate you from your prejudices, so that you are guided solely by his truth and love.

## Self responsibility

In listening, beware of giving advice, even when asked to do so. You do not put your beliefs into a drawer when you help others, far from it. But it is essential to help other people take responsibility for their own decisions. The depressed personality often finds decision making extremely hard. It is good, therefore, to help a person come to this point by clarifying as far as possible what are the options open for them in a particular situation. They must then make a choice based on those options. There is no law against giving advice, but it is important to help people take full responsibility for their own lives.

There has to be a sensible balance in all this. This will particularly be so when living with someone who is depressed. Since the ability and confidence to make decisions can be particularly impaired by depression, try wherever possible to assist the person in making their own decisions. Though the last thing the depressed person needs is badgering or undue pressure, they may need a helping hand or even a push. But they will gain confidence and self respect from taking such responsibility for themselves. Of course, it is perfectly acceptable to relieve the burden of decision making in some ways, but the severely depressed need reminding they are worthwhile persons, who can win through and return to normal, whole and fulfilled lives. The achievement of even minor goals of decision making can help in this.

## Caring for friends and family

Depression can be an exhausting experience for sufferer and carer alike. It is important that carers, whether friends or family, take seriously the suggestions for effective self care for themselves. Warm acceptance is important for the depressed person, but there comes a point when everybody's reserves of strength begin to wane. You may want to scream with frustration that the person you love or care for is as they are at the moment, and does not seem to be making any progress at all. It is indeed deeply frustrating.

Carers also need carers, so try and find someone to listen to *you*. It may be your minister, doctor, friend or neighbour. But you cannot be the 'strong' one all of the time. In the majority of cases so much can be done for depression. If you are not satisfied with the help you are receiving, go and seek further advice. Keep praying for the depressed person and yourself. Get others to pray with you too. Try and get a break or a holiday. Keep a watch on your own diet, exercise, spiritual life, sociability, emotions and attitudes, personal planning, and self encouragement.

Self help and the helping of others comes down to some basics of good common sense. If we live, respecting the dynamics of the way which God has created us, we are far more likely to do well when gloom approaches us, or someone close to us. We are responsible for ourselves, and it is only too easy to neglect what is important; but the solution is just as easily within our grasp.

## 14

# FINDING FREEDOM

How can we find freedom when circumstances overwhelm and depress us, and when so much seems against us? Is there any approach to facing up to depression which combines both the spiritual and the practical; an approach which will not only lend us support in times of difficulty, but will enable us to sail against the tide and overcome?

A spiritual approach which aims to see the involvement of the living God in all of life's circumstances will aim for a vital reorientation of world-view, values, attitudes and understanding of faith; yet such a reorientation implies an equally practical outworking in terms of everyday planning for healthy and fulfilled living, with the personal aims, goals and strategy that reorientation necessitates. Aspirations become actions when we close the gap between good ideas and the decision making they imply.

It is indeed important that we aim not simply to deal with the symptoms of our inner discomforts, but to learn new patterns of responding to life's tensions, hurdles and difficulties. This transformation of life is central to the new way of living for followers of Jesus Christ. This is why the New Testament so often responds to actual situations of pressure and discomfort which themselves contain all the agonising possibilities of a thoroughly depressive response. The example of Paul's prison letters is highly illuminating in this respect, particularly his letter to the Philippians, which provides both spiritual and practical principles for 'freedom within the storm'.

## A new perspective

How we see what we see makes a big impact on our spirits. Waking up to a gloomy, grey day can be annoyingly miserable if you have nothing to do or look forward to that day or that week; but the greyness of the weather will matter little to you if tomorrow you are due to fly out to somewhere beautiful to spend a glorious fortnight in the sun.

It is possible to react quite differently to the very same circumstances. When it comes to adversity, the Bible shows us examples of constructive responses which make very much more of the situation than the circumstances might initially suggest. Once again in the example of the Apostle Paul, we see a spiritual approach to overcoming which is vitally alive in terms of world-view, values, attitudes and faith expressed in prayer. 'Yes, and I will continue to rejoice, for I know that through your prayers and the help given by the Spirit of Jesus Christ, what has happened to me will turn out for my deliverance' (Philippians 1:18, 19).

Here is a different perspective on circumstances. Paul is in prison. It is not absolutely certain exactly where, for he served at least four known prison sentences during this period – in Philippi itself, in Jerusalem, Caesarea and Rome – but many contemporary historians believe that Rome was the most likely place. You can visit the Mamartine prison in Rome today, as many tourists do. It is well documented that both Paul and the Apostle Peter were imprisoned there at different times. Though the prison is no longer in use, it is still possible to see how appalling the conditions actually were. To perceive how dreadful was Paul's situation helps all the more to appreciate how vitally he adjusted his perspectives and outlook as to what was happening to him.

The Mamartine prison is below ground. As you enter it by descending some stairs, you first come to a small circular chamber where the Praetorian guard would have been on constant duty. Below, there is nothing much more than a hole in the ground, about eight feet wide and twelve feet high;

a tiny space, with no light, and an earthen floor. This is where Paul the Apostle would have been chained to his guard. From this situation he wrote his letter to the Philippians, dictating it to one of his visitors who would have been allowed upstairs to speak to him through the grill, which was the kind of trap door to his cell below.

When we think of night and day lived out in such discomfort, it is difficult to imagine anything more depressing or more likely to dampen the spirit. It is in just these situations that we are most likely to quickly lose our sparkle and enthusiasm, and to begin to question the goodness of God and his purpose for us; perhaps even to conclude that God is powerless to help.

Paul's perspective on his circumstances is, then, all the more striking. 'Yes I shall rejoice. For I know that through your prayers and the help of the spirit of Jesus Christ, this will turn out for my deliverance.'

It is an attitude remarkable for its constructiveness. When Paul says 'This will turn out for my deliverance', the Greek word he uses is *soteria*. It is the normal word for salvation. Deliverance doesn't mean he is expecting to get out of prison, but that in prison he will find a new kind of freedom, which is part of the richness of the salvation which Jesus Christ brings irrespective of our circumstances.

So often we would rather have a quick and simple deliverance from the situations which depress us, but it is what we make of those situations while we are in them which really counts.

* Review your own situation. What is your present perspective on your circumstances?
* Do you need to revise your perspective?
* Are there any spiritual or other factors which you should be taking into account to help you in this?

## Opportunity knocks

Whatever the situation there will always be opportunities to effect something worthwhile, if we will only keep our eyes open to purposeful activity. Everyone needs to guard against the hedgehog response. Rolling ourselves up in a ball at the slightest sign of danger by withdrawing from the challenges of the outside world may feel comforting for a while; but the hedgehog who heard the lorry coming unfortunately found it an ineffective defence. When the pressure hots up, withdrawal is not necessarily the best way of coping. The use of opportunities, by contrast, helps you to climb out of the emotional restrictions of your situation.

If we learn healthy habits of life while we are able, then we will have greatly increased strength for the particularly testing times we may face. Paul always used his opportunities to the full, when his life was at its most 'normal'. In prison, he did just the same. It is clear from the Philippians letter that the whole Praetorian guard knew about Paul's faith in Christ. Paul talked about Christ to people around him. This was *his* use of opportunity. You might think for Paul the cost would be particularly high; this is one of the reasons he was in prison in the first place. You may think you couldn't choose a worse place to evangelise; yet Paul is saying, 'Don't you see, people are becoming Christians. God is using me, and all this is part of the salvation process, to be used by God. It is turning out for my salvation.'

The main point to grasp is this use of opportunity in general. In Paul's case, it was the opportunity for evangelism. But wherever we are and in whatever circumstances, God will provide a specific opportunity to be used in his service. This does not have to be anything overtly 'spiritual' at all; most often it will be a matter of doing something simply useful and worthwhile, and plainly within your ability at that time to do it.

We cannot get away from the basic spiritual truth about purpose. God saves us to use us. We see that Paul is letting

himself be used in spite of his adverse circumstances. It is a
question of perspective. A normal estimation of his circumstances might conclude, 'this is a disaster – nothing worse
could happen to me.' But what does Paul know which makes
the difference to this kind of possible reaction? Paul knows
that God is always at work in us. He never gives up. His
purposes will never be defeated, however hemmed in we may
feel, humanly speaking. 'Being confident of this, that he who
began a good work in you will carry it on to completion until
the day of Jesus Christ' (Philippians 1:6).

We all tend to put environment or circumstances very high
on our list of what has to be 'right' if we are to feel 'good'. But
here we encounter an opposite claim. In a sense, circumstances are irrelevant, certainly of far less importance, as
long as you are prepared to let God use you – and for you to
take up your opportunities when they are there.

* What makes you want to withdraw, hedgehog-like, from
  possible 'danger'?
* Should you be learning new patterns of more purposeful
  use of opportunities?
* What practical, manageable task could you take on at the
  moment to give yourself something purposeful outside
  your present situation?

It is God's strength in you, not your strength in yourself
which matters. You'll find the opportunities right on your
own doorstep. Start where you are.

## Confidence in God

In depression, personal and spiritual confidence become
quickly eroded. Yet felt confidence is less important than the
actual trustworthiness of God. What we feel about God is less

important than what we know about him. I know my wife loves me because she says so, and I know she wouldn't say it if she did not mean it. More so, she has demonstrated her love in so many practical ways. If I wake up one dull day and wonder about her love, ('Is it real, does she really love me?') I need to fall back on what I know and not on what I feel. Feelings are an unreliable guide to the true reality of things. It is the same with our faith in God. The true basis of spiritual confidence involves prayer and the help of the Spirit, all of which comes to us as we steadily draw on the truth about God and his ways which we learn from his word. It is only when we actively come to seek God's help in this way that problems are transformed into genuine opportunities. 'I know that through your prayers and the help given by the Spirit of Jesus Christ, what has happened to me will turn out for my deliverance' (Philippians 1:19).

Paul speaks about what he *knows*. His conviction is based upon the facts about God and how he has seen God at work. It is valuable to reflect on whether we have that same confidence as Paul in prayer and the Spirit. Paul was quite clearly having a tough time; and yet as we have already seen, a touch of adversity is a great perspective restorer.

None of us would wish discomfort or suffering on anyone directly. But God sometimes uses such experience to change us positively, and a great problem in these days of affluence and anaesthetics, is that some people can be isolated from any doubts about their actual security for many years, before they face up to the fragility of life and existence.

Often you'll hear someone say they are quite prepared for other people to be Christians, but don't feel any need within, to justify themselves becoming a Christian. It is a common enough remark, especially in the affluent Western world. Our lives and environment can feel comfortably secure in many ways, with enough money, enough food, enough Hi Fi, enough clout to be pretty steady in life.

Sad to tell, that kind of security is an illusion. It is not that we are not meant to enjoy the good things we have; but our

lives have serious cracks in them. When we stop to think
about it we know it's true. We feel it when we lose loved ones.
We also feel it as we get older and our bodies begin to decline.
Is life meant to be like this? Are we designed inevitably to run
out of steam, to decay and die? Or has something gone wrong
and do we need God's aid?

Go it alone and ignore God, and the Bible insists sadly
there is calamity ahead. Take up God's offer of help, and a
new start is offered to anyone who will turn from a self
centred life, to a Christ centred life. But having taken up
God's offer of help, if you continue without genuine prayer
and reliance on the Spirit, then life will not be calamitous,
but it will be fruitless. For prayer is meant to be the very life
blood of our involvement with God.

* Is there a prayer centre to your life?
* Do you need to begin or develop your prayer relationship
  with God?

Paul had learnt the secret of prayer when his life was at its
most productive. In certain kinds and depths of depression, it
can be very difficult to pray. But when you are back to
normal, will you aim to learn this secret of strength
and power and being in tune with God's purposes for
you?

## Develop purpose

Without a sense of purpose, we easily become dejected.
Depression itself brings feelings of purposelessness. In his
letter to the Philippians, Paul makes one of the greatest
affirmations of purpose ever recorded, and its substance is
highly instructive. 'For to me, to live is Christ and to die is

gain' (Philippians 1:21). Paul has written of his sense of being
used by God, even in adverse circumstances, as part of the
salvation process; but there is a further dimension still. Later
Paul says, 'I have learned to be content whatever the circumstances' (Philippians 4:11). That secret seems to be
dependent on his sense of purpose, 'For to me, to live is
Christ and to die is gain'. Paul is a remarkable example of
singlemindedness of purpose.

Os Guiness once said that one of the greatest weaknesses
amongst Christians today is lack of singlemindedness. Put
round the other way, that implies the presence of double
mindedness. It is important to ask ourselves searching questions on this point, for our answers will affect our wholeness,
and any under-surface conflict we may be facing.

If you are in business or at home as a housewife or you
work in a profession or whether you are not working at all,
are you double minded? When you are with Christians you
speak about spiritual things, there is a real sincerity, but is
there a yawning gap between what you say and what you
do? When you get to work and you are dealing with something in a non Christian setting do you cease to behave as a
Christian?

Does the gap show in that you don't pray about family,
friends and colleagues; you don't seek God's help to apply
your faith to the specific issues you face at work or home;
neither do you seek the help of other Christians to work out
specific questions which apply to your situation? Measure
yourself by Paul's example. Paul says 'for me to live is
Christ.' It is an undivided sense of purpose. So all of us must
learn not to privatise our belief, and not to compartmentalise
our faith, because Jesus Christ wants to affect the whole of
our lives, as he did for Paul. It is the way to reduce our stock
of inner conflict, and iron out the creases in our Christian
integrity, because living for Christ involves the totality of our
experience. Such points of consistency of approach are positive encouragements for growth, and make a great deal of
difference to our sense of achievement, self image, and overall
worth and direction in life.

## Attitudes to death

You don't have to live long before you encounter death in a
loved one. However, for most people the affairs of every day
quite soon provide distractions from the nagging uncertainties of mortality which these sad times bring. Death is the
great unmentionable of today. How different is this attitude
from the eras which have preceded ours. 'Do you know how
to die?' The Puritan teachers asked that question regularly,
for they were much concerned about what they called 'a good
death'. It is important for us too that we ask ourselves the
same question, whether we are prepared for death, for our
answer will make such a difference to our outlook, values and
goals, and indeed to our inner fears and priorities.

Is the whole subject of death for you a morbid thought,
something you'd rather not think about? But unless you have
come to terms with death, you cannot really come to terms
with life. Measure your own thoughts against these words of
Paul, 'to die is gain'. If you believe that is true, in what ways
should it affect your values, your directions, your use of the
wealth and the gifts God has given you, as well as the
opportunities which are before you? 'To die is gain', char-
acterises Paul's clear sense of purpose, and we are encouraged to measure ourselves against that understanding of
purpose and direction in life.

* Have you faced up to the issue of your own mortality?
* What can Paul's words, 'to die is gain', come to mean to
  you?

## Establish goals

We all need goals. Yet in depression the sense of purpose can
be so diminished that directions and targets quickly become

ignored. Sadly the effect is cyclical. The less the emphasis on purposeful activity, the greater the sense of slowing down and stagnation. It is all the more important to be clear about establishing goals.

What was Paul aiming at in his ministry to the Philippians? What were his goals? The awareness of goals is hinted at when he says 'I know . . . I will continue with all of you for your progress and joy in the faith' (Philippians 1:25). The goals are in the phrase 'your progress and joy'. Paul was quite obviously an achiever. He knew precisely where he was going and that is why he accomplished so much. He wanted the Philippians to make progress and to know joy in their faith in Christ. What can we learn from his goal orientation?

A high street store undergoing alterations and improvements put up a sign in front of the shop, simply saying 'Pardon our progress'. The word 'progress' sometimes causes problems; some people are almost instinctively apologetic about it.

Paul is not apologetic about the need for progress for the Philippians; he is positively concerned for their 'progress and [their] joy in the faith'. The word Paul uses for progress is revealing. *Prokope* literally means 'striking forward'. It was originally used of a pioneer cutting his way through brushwood. Paul links joy in the faith of Christ with this kind of progress. When we are striking forward and breaking new ground as Christians, then we will know joy. This means reviewing our perspectives, using our opportunities, all the while relying upon God in prayer, based upon a clear sense of purpose.

* What kinds of goals should you set yourself to make progress spiritually?
* Take some time to use the goal setting exercise below to develop an approach to setting goals for your own life and situation.

## Goal setting

It is essential for good spiritual self management that we change aspirations into decisions for action. So often we will say to ourselves that something sounds a good idea or something would be nice, helpful or a step forward, but then manifestly fail to do anything concrete about it. What we have learned from Paul is that he was spiritually a man of action. He refused to become engulfed by circumstances. We too can become so much more energetically decisive if we adopt an analytical approach to our desire to take purposeful action on our own behalf. The tension between the desirable and the actual is formed by barriers which may well be overcome once they have been accurately identified and an action plan has been formulated.

| IDEAL GOAL | ACTUAL EXPERIENCE | BARRIERS | ACTION PLAN |
| --- | --- | --- | --- |
| To develop my spiritual life through prayer and Bible study. | I read the Bible with little understanding and I pray hardly at all. I have been slow in getting involved with a church Bible study group, and tend to fall asleep at night before praying. | I am lazy about organising things. I don't like praying at night anyway. | I will phone up the leader of the house groups at my church by the end of the week to arrange to join a group. I will set my alarm half an hour earlier in the mornings to have a time to pray when I am fresh. |

Personal goal setting exercise example

This example shows that in any attempt to establish effective goals we must give our attention to the ideal, the actual experience, the barriers and then an action plan. Sometimes we will mentally go through the following steps as a natural, spontaneous process. It is instructive, however, to go about this in a more considered way, writing down the steps on paper to encourage a more rigorous analysis, and a heightened sense of decision once the action plan has been committed to paper.

## These are the steps outlined a little more fully

### The ideal goal

This means realistically identifying the ideal goal or objective for your situation, assuming that all factors including yourself are functioning at maximum effectiveness. (They won't be, but we are talking here about the ideal only.) Ask what would be happening if you were functioning in a fully effective way, and what would *not* be happening too.

### The actual experience

What is currently being achieved? Describe briefly what is happening now, the actual experience in your situation.

### Barriers

This is the gap between the ideal and the actual. What is it that is preventing you from realistically putting the ideal goal into practice? What are the barriers? Asking these questions will reveal much which gets in the way of your effective functioning.

The questions will involve:

**Ability:** 'Do I need to learn anything?' This is to do with skill, knowledge, and experience.

**Willingness:** 'Do I need to change my behaviour or attitude?' This is to do with your own willingness to make changes and move forward.

**Behaviour of others:** 'Do I need to persuade others to

change their behaviour or attitude, or to co-operate with me in some way?' This is to do with relationships.

**Action:** 'Do I need to do something specific?' This is to do with actual possible courses of action open to you.

*Action plan*

This will need to correspond to the ideal and what you need to do to overcome the barriers you have identified. Your action plan needs to be specific and not general, and to include a time setting for each planned objective.

* Now try the personal goal setting exercise for yourself.
* Choose some important personal issue where you need to make progress.
* Take each step in turn.
* Keep it manageable.
* Put it into practice!
* Aim to apply these steps of personal planning to all the elements you have discovered about yourself while reading and thinking about the exercises and ideas in these pages, especially where you know you need to see progress. Don't do them all in one go, but make a list, and take them at a reasonable daily or weekly pace.
* With these wider goals in mind, don't forget the importance of the small practical goals which need to be set regularly every day, to give you a sense of achievement. Just making up your mind to cook a proper meal or take an hour's exercise will help your sense of fulfilment as well as contributing to your general health and well being.

Establishing clear, manageable and relevant goals is an important element in developing an active spirituality which will strengthen and sustain in times of difficulty and stress. Such an approach, to give direction, purpose, and strength is most effectively used when the worst depressive phase has passed. But to have a clear and thoughtfully worked out plan of action for your life will maintain you in the difficult times, and provide one more element of effective protection in your personal and emotional self management.

# Postscript

# 15

# THE OTHER SIDE OF THE TUNNEL

Depression is a wretched experience for anyone to face. As we have seen, there are a wide variety of depressive conditions, ranging from the out of sorts to the grossly debilitating. If you have picked up this book and you are unfortunate enough to be facing depression now in some form, I want to aim to encourage you realistically.

Depression saps your energy, self esteem, sense of purpose and any joy in living you used to know. It may be difficult for you to believe this at the moment, but your life may not be exactly as you feel it to be. The horrid thing about depression is that it makes everything seem far blacker than it actually is. You may not think it is possible for anything to change, but it is indeed possible. You can get better, if you decide to take the help which is at hand.

Much of what is contained in this book is designed to help you when you are feeling somewhat better, to prevent recurring symptoms. You'll find it valuable to do the exercises and link up the insights with practical action. Right now you may well need help from friends, family or professional sources. The help which is available to you above all is the help which comes from God. 'The Lord is my Shepherd, I shall lack nothing . . . Even though I walk through the valley of the shadow of death, I will fear no evil, for you are with me' (Psalm 23:1, 4).

In all your difficulties, can you remember this? God loves you with a depth and passion of concern that it is scarcely possible for us humanly to understand. Through Jesus Christ and his death on the cross, he completely forgives you for all the wrong in your life and offers the power and joy of his Holy

Spirit to be your daily companion and strength. If you will
make up your mind to do what is necessary for your contribution to your healing, to face the underlying elements giving
rise to your depression, God himself will supply whatever it is
your need determines. Do believe it, for there is another side
to the tunnel.

So many who have suffered know the relief the experience
of freedom brings. You can too. Don't despair; be active in
doing whatever you can to help yourself, and seeking the help
of others suitably qualified to help you. Above all put your
trust in the one who loves you, and gave his son to die for you.

'For I know the plans I have for you,' declares the Lord,
'plans to prosper you and not to harm you, plans to give you
hope and a future. Then you will call upon me and come
and pray to me, and I will listen to you. You will seek me
and find me when you seek me with all your heart.'

[Jeremiah 29:11–13]